Checote's Angels

A True Story of a Horse, a Miracle, and the Angels Who Surrounded Us

A Memoir by *Tammy Holsey*

Copyright Page

Checote's Angels:
A True Story of a Horse, a Miracle, and the Angels Who Surrounded Us

This is a work of nonfiction. The events described in this memoir reflect the author's experiences and recollections. Certain names and identifying details may have been changed to respect the privacy of individuals.

ISBN: 979-8-9939754-2-9
First Edition: **2025**
Printed in the United States of America

Cover design and artwork by Tamara J. Holsey

About This Book

Checote's Angels tells the true story of a horse whose life was guided by unseen hands, and the woman who learned to hear the whispers between worlds.

When a young wild horse named Checote is rescued from a terrible accident that should have been fatal, he begins a healing journey filled with messages, miracles, and the presence of angels that only the open-hearted can sense. Through animal communicators, uncanny intuition, and inexplicable moments of grace, Tammy discovers that her beloved horse is surrounded – protected – by angels who never leave his side.

Together, they face devastating injuries, near-death infections, hornet attacks, heartbreak, betrayal, and the kind of grief that bends the soul. But through every challenge, Checote's love shines through with absolute clarity. His loyalty is fierce. His spirit is ancient. And his mission is greater than either of them ever understood.

This is more than a memoir – it is a testament to the unseen connections between humans and animals, the angels who walk beside us, and the extraordinary ways a single horse can change a life forever.

Dedication

To Checote, who showed me what it means to listen with the heart…

and to every reader who has ever loved an animal with the kind of love that changes your life forever.

Table of Contents

Foreword

Every once in a while, a horse comes along who changes **more** than the way we ride – he changes the way we live. Checote was one of those rare souls. He was more than a companion on the trail; he was a teacher, a healer, and a mirror reflecting the truest parts of the human heart. His story is not just about the miles he traveled, the water he swam, or the wild beginnings that shaped him. It is about loyalty, trust, resilience, and the kind of quiet wisdom only a horse can give.

In these pages, meet Checote through the eyes of someone who loved him deeply and walked beside him through triumphs, heartbreaks, and the tender moments that linger long after a hoofprint fades. An unlikely horse, born running wild on a Texas ranch, becomes a steadfast partner and a cherished friend. He gave everything he had – until the day he gently asked to be let go.

This is more than the story of a horse's life; it is the story of a bond that shaped a journey. It is a reminder that the relationships we build with animals can be some of the most meaningful and transformative in our lives.

A true horse partner doesn't just carry our weight – they carry our soul.

Checote did that. And through this book, he still does.

Chapter One – The Horse Who Changed My Life

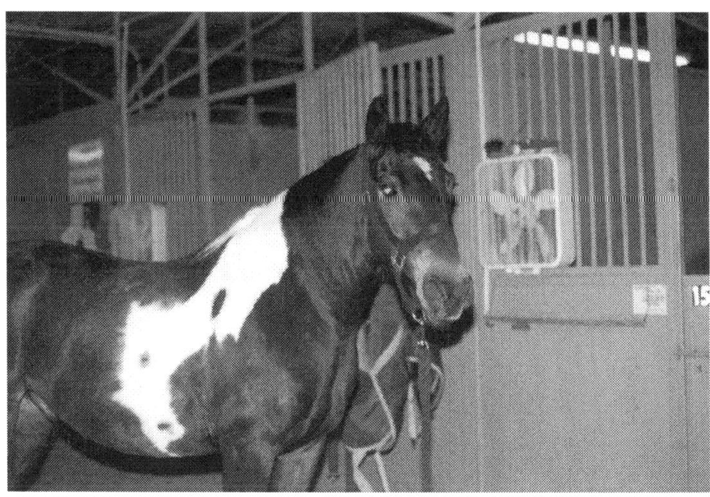

Checote's First Picture

This is the story of my horse, – Checote (chuh-KOH-tee) – the horse who changed my life. He wasn't just my companion and riding partner; he was my best friend.

Checote's story began on a quiet stretch of Texas land, not far from Houston, where a small band of wild horses ran free across a private ranch. The owner, Henry Taub, often donated a few of them each year to the Houston Farm & Ranch Club charity auction that raised money for local causes.

George Love – known to most folks as *Indian George* – was the man trusted to capture those wild horses, bring them home, and gentle them for thirty days before the auction.

Among that year's herd was a young pinto with a bright eye and a quick spirit – Checote. Though he had known only the wind and open range, he took kindly to people. He was one of the easiest horses that Indian George had ever trained. He accepted the saddle without fear, and on his very first ride in the round pen, he did what he loved most – he ran.

Round and round he went, as fast as he could, and yet he never bucked. That was Checote's way: wild at heart, but steady and kind.

When the charity auction came around, my friend Tom Dompier placed the winning bid. Tom owned a six-thousand-acre working cattle ranch on the outskirts of Houston. For a while, the ranch hands called the little horse *Ole Paint*. But at just fourteen hands high, he was too small for the work and too short for the big men who rode him. Because of that, he wasn't ridden or used very often. He spent his days quietly – standing in the pasture, overlooked and unused. He rarely carried riders, but he carried something deeper: patience, purpose, and a quiet knowing that his story wasn't meant to end there.

When Checote Chose Me

Around that same time, I was facing the heartbreak of retiring my Quarter Horse, Leah. After years of trail rides and long days together, a stifle injury ended her riding days. Because of her bloodlines, a friend offered to use her as a broodmare, and I began the search for a new horse – though my heart wasn't sure it was ready.

In February of 1999, while riding the Salt Grass Trail Ride, I mentioned to Tom that I was looking for another mount. He smiled and said, "I've got a little pinto you might like."

He told me about the horse who once tangled his leg in a rope and had simply stood still, waiting patiently for help. "He's got the kind of temperament that makes a great riding horse," Tom said. "Calm, steady, trusting."

I didn't know it yet, but that horse would become the heart of my story – and the keeper of my soul.

A month later, I met Checote for the first time. From the moment I saw him, something stirred inside me – a quiet recognition, like meeting an old friend you hadn't seen in years. There was no hesitation, no nerves, just an unspoken understanding. I felt completely at peace beside him.

That day, I climbed on his back, and it was as if we had been riding together all our lives. In that instant, our bond was sealed – a silent agreement between two souls who somehow already knew they belonged to one another.

From that moment on, Checote and I began our journey together. What started as a simple meeting between a woman and a small, wild-hearted horse grew into something much deeper – a partnership built on trust, patience, and quiet understanding. Every time I looked into his eyes, I felt as though he already knew what I was thinking.

I couldn't have imagined then just how far we would go together – or how much this little pinto would impact my heart and my life.

A New Beginning

When I brought Checote home, it felt like the whole world finally exhaled with me. Losing Leah as my riding partner had left a quiet ache I couldn't quite name. I wasn't sure I'd ever find another horse who understood me the way she did. And then, there he was

– a small, beautifully marked pinto with calm eyes that seemed to say, *You can trust me.*

The first few days, I spent more time just being near him than trying to ride. I'd stand by the fence and watch him move – the way his tail swished lazily in the breeze, how his ears flicked toward every sound but never in fear. There was a quiet confidence about him, a steadiness I hadn't expected in a horse that had once run wild.

When I finally slipped a halter over his head and led him out, he followed willingly, as if he'd been waiting for that moment too. His steps were light and measured beside me, his head lowered just enough to show respect, but not submission. I spoke to him softly, calling his name, and each time I said *Checote*, he flicked an ear as though he recognized it.

That first ride was as smooth and honest as any I'd ever had. He stood still while I mounted, then walked out with a purpose, his stride sure and balanced. When I asked him to trot, he lifted into it easily, ears forward, waiting for my next cue. There was no testing, no stubbornness – just quiet understanding. I remember thinking, *He's not just carrying me – he's listening.*

When he ran, his hooves barely seemed to touch the earth. It was his joy, and mine. In those moments, with the wind in my face and his mane whipping around me, I would think, *Maybe you really can fly without ever leaving the ground.*

As we rode, I couldn't help but notice how different he was from Leah. Where she had been spirited and strong-willed, Checote was patient and thoughtful. His strength was quieter, more grounded. He sensed, somehow, that what I needed wasn't power or performance – but peace, and a place to heal.

By the time we returned to the barn that day, something had changed inside me. The sadness I'd carried for so long began to lift, replaced by a quiet joy I hadn't felt in months. I didn't need to search anymore – I had found my partner.

From that moment forward, Checote wasn't just my horse. He was my heart on four legs.

Running at Sister Creek Ranch

The Bond Between Us

Checote and I went on countless trail rides together, each one an adventure in its own right. Over the years, our connection deepened until it felt unbreakable – a quiet understanding that didn't need words. Somewhere along the miles of open trails, we developed our own language. A shift of my weight, a soft breath, or the slightest touch of the reins was all it took. He seemed to sense my thoughts before I spoke them, and I could feel his moods just as clearly.

We put down miles the way some people say prayers. Trail after trail, hour after hour, until the rhythm of his hooves replaced the noise of life with something simple and true.

There were days when we'd ride for hours in silence, the rhythm of his hooves and the whisper of the wind were the only sounds between us. Sometimes he'd flick an ear back toward me as if to say, *You doing okay back there?* And I'd smile, knowing he already knew the answer.

My husband was a city boy and land was never in his plans, so boarding became our way of life. It turned out to be a blessing. Barns have their own kind of neighborhood – conversations in tack rooms, laughter in aisleways, friendships forged over late-night colics and early-morning rides. I found my people there: as horse-crazy as I am, happy to measure seasons by mud, flies, and rodeo dates.

One of our favorite traditions was riding in the **Houston Livestock Show and Rodeo Trail Rides** each year. The one we always rode was the **Salt Grass Trail Ride** – a week-long journey full of laughter, long days in the saddle, and the spirit of Texas. Checote loved it. He thrived on the energy and excitement, but most of all, he loved the people – especially the children.

Whenever we passed a crowd, his head would lift a little higher and his prance would get just a bit more animated, as if he knew he was putting on a show. He soaked up every bit of attention, ears perked and eyes bright. Checote wasn't just part of the ride – he was part of the joy.

Salt Grass Trail Ride

Checote always made sure I was safe. He never did anything that would cause me to lose my balance or fall. Some of the barns where we boarded had wonderful riding trails, but it was up to us to keep them trimmed back and passable. A group of us would set a day to work on the trails, riding out with clippers, trimmers, and even saws tied to our saddles.

On one of those trail-trimming days, I came across a branch that had grown so low it was impossible to ride under without getting knocked off. To reach the part that needed cutting, I had to stand up in the saddle. I asked Checote to stop beneath the tree, grabbed my loppers, and carefully rose to my feet on his back. As I began cutting, a few of the limbs dropped right onto him – some even hitting him on the head. But Checote didn't move a muscle. He stood as still as a statue, calm and steady, keeping me safe until the last branch was cleared.

In that moment, I realized just how deep our trust ran. He trusted me to lead him, and I trusted him with my life – and neither of us ever let the other down.

As the years went by, Checote became more than just my riding partner – he became my anchor. No matter what was happening in my life, I could always count on him to bring me peace. There was something healing about the time we spent together, the quiet rhythm of grooming him after a long day, or the gentle weight of his breath on my shoulder when I leaned close.

He seemed to know when I was sad or troubled. On those days, he would rest his head against me, his eyes soft and patient, as if to say, *It's okay – we've got this.* I never had to speak; he just knew. Horses like Checote don't come along often – the kind who understand your heart without needing a single word.

Our rides were joyful. The world seemed to fade away once I was in the saddle. With each steady stride, I could feel any worries of the day melt into the wind. Whether we were trotting down familiar trails or exploring new ones, it was always the same sense of freedom – two souls moving as one.

Carrying the Flag

Two Old Souls

The first time I took my dog Tanner – a Husky/Shepherd mix – on a trail ride, we were at George Slater's eight-hundred-acre ranch in Orchard, Texas. Big sky, bigger heat. If I'd known how hot it would get, I might've left Tanner home. He had never gone on a trail ride with us before, and this was going to be his "big adventure."

We set out – my step-sister, Rachael, on Sister; her mother, Mary, on Coco; Sallie on Wednesday; George on his gelding; and me on Checote. Tanner wanted to lead but didn't know the way, so he planted himself right in front of us, turning to stare up at me like, *Why are you up there?* He was one step from getting stepped on.

I told Checote firmly, "Do *not* step on Tanner." And he listened. More than once, he stopped mid-stride, one hoof frozen in the air, just to keep from touching Tanner. Eventually, I convinced Tanner that it was safer to walk beside us instead of in front.

Two hours later, the heat caught him. The eager trot turned to a stagger, chest heaving, paws clumsy. As we approached the barn, a stock tank shimmered ahead like a promise. I slid off, scooped Tanner up, and dropped him into the water.

He stood there, belly deep, sides heaving, while I splashed water over his back again and again. The others watched for a few moments, making sure Tanner was stabilizing, then decided to continue to the barn to get out of the sun.

I didn't realize they'd left until the silence settled. I wasn't even holding the reins; they were looped over the saddle horn. I finally looked up, everyone was gone – everyone except Checote. He was still there, head down inside the tank, watching Tanner like a worried brother.

Coco and Sister – his “girls” – had gone on without him, but Checote never made a move to follow. He stayed with Tanner and me, watching, waiting.

When Tanner had his legs under him again, I lifted him out, made sure he was steady, climbed back in the saddle, and turned for the barn. I braced for the rush – Checote is buddy-sour with his girls, and the herd was out of sight – but he walked slower than I’ve ever felt him walk. Slow enough for a tired dog to keep up at a comfortable amble. Step for step, he matched Tanner all the way to the barn.

From that day on, Tanner and Checote were inseparable friends. Tanner came with us on many adventures after that, and Checote always knew exactly where he was. When we had to cross a busy road, Tanner would tuck himself close under my left stirrup, and Checote would slow his stride again – careful, protective, watchful – making sure his friend crossed safely.

They understood each other in a way that only old souls do.

Watching Checote and Tanner together taught me something about loyalty and friendship that no person ever could teach me. Their friendship wasn’t built on words or commands – it was built on quiet understanding, trust, and pure heart.

Checote never had to be told to look after Tanner; he just did. And Tanner, in his own way, trusted that Checote would always be there for him. They understood each other without being taught. Loyalty doesn’t always bark or whinny. Sometimes it just…walks with you at your pace.

Even now, when I think back on all the trails we’ve ridden, the image that stays with me most clearly is that of my horse and my dog – two loyal souls, moving together through the world, and each watching over me.

Tanner Cooling Off In The Stock Tank

The J&S Swim Team

There were a handful of us that boarded our horses at J&S Ranch in Cypress, Texas, who loved riding together, and did so regularly. We typically ended up laughing until our sides hurt, and we supported each other through everything – from sick or injured horses to illness and life's heartbreaks. And sometimes… we accidentally created memories none of us ever stopped talking about.

Memorial Day weekend was one of those times.

Four of us decided to trailer our horses to Jones Forest State Park for a long, carefree day ride. There was Sallie with her beautiful (but often funny) Quarter Horse, Wednesday; Gwen and her sweet mare, Fancy; twelve-year-old Rachael and her retired roping horse, Sister; and me – Tammy – with my loyal Pinto, Checote, and my dog Tanner, who was convinced that Cote was his best friend, and he therefore went where Checote went.

Tanner rides shotgun like he owns the truck, and I swear he understands every word I say. He knows when I'm loading the truck to go to the barn, and there's no way he's staying behind.

When we pulled into the parking area at Jones Forest, it already felt warm, but none of us realized we were about to ride straight into a steam sauna disguised as a forest. South Texas humidity doesn't play – it sneaks up on you, grabs you by the throat, and says, "Welcome to summer, sweetheart!"

Once saddled, we set off into the wide, sandy trails. The forest was beautiful – birds everywhere, rabbits darting like tiny athletes, and even deer gracefully judging us from the distant trees. We walked, trotted, loped, and laughed through the dust. Within minutes, every single one of us looked like we'd been dipped in sweat and rolled in powdered sugar.

As Texans, we're used to this heat. But even we have limits.

Thank God for the ponds.

After an hour of riding, we reached the first one. The horses marched straight into the water like they'd been dreaming of it. Tanner dove in with the confidence of an Olympic swimmer who'd never actually been in deep water before.

The horses started pawing and splashing, sending glorious cold water onto our burning legs. It took exactly ten seconds before we all looked at each other and said, "Saddles off?"

Saddles off.

I had a secret agenda. I wanted Checote to swim. I hadn't swum with a horse since my childhood pony in the old pasture pond – and if you've ever swam with a horse, you know there's nothing like it.

Swimming with a horse feels like riding strength made weightless. The moment his hooves leave the ground, everything goes quiet – no hoofbeats, no dust, just water and breath. His powerful body becomes light and fluid beneath you, gliding instead of stepping. You feel his trust, his rhythm, his calm.

You're not just riding him – you're floating *with* him.

So, Sallie, Rachael, and I stripped off boots, socks, and anything not waterproof. The moment that hot, thick Texas air touched my bare feet… I almost proposed marriage to the breeze. Meanwhile, Gwen announced she was staying dry, staying onshore, and taking pictures. This was perfect because I needed evidence of whatever nonsense was about to happen.

Barefoot and bareback, we rode into the pond. The horses walked in without hesitation, loving every second. The water soaked our jeans, cooled our feet, and turned us into giggling school girls. We splashed, laughed, and clung to our horses' manes like we were part of some backwoods mermaid tribe.

And then there was Tanner.
Lord help him.

He swam from horse to horse, trying to figure out why his large four-legged friends were in the water. At one point, he swam up to Wednesday, planted himself nose-to-nose, and gave him a big, soggy dog kiss. Wednesday's expression said very clearly: *"I did not sign up for this."*

After about twenty minutes of play, we dried off enough to re-saddle and ate lunch. Still dripping wet, we sat in the shade, laughing over everything. The kind of laughter that warms your ribs and stays with you for years.

After lunch, we rode deeper into the forest, finding new trails and pushing through brush thick enough that Checote basically blazed his own path. He led like a champion, ears up, chest out – my proud Pinto determined to be the explorer of the day.

On the way back, we stopped at our favorite pond again. And this is where things escalated.

We pulled off the saddles again, splashed around… and then Sallie and I shared That Look.

The "Are we going to do something stupid and unforgettable?" look.

"Yes. Yes, we are."

We decided to actually swim the horses – really swim them – across the pond.

We rode to the far side, bareback, barefoot, hearts pounding with excitement. Then, one by one, we entered the water. Chest-deep… belly-deep… and then suddenly –

Over their heads.

The moment their hooves lost the bottom, the horses did what horses do – they bobbed straight up and down like giant one-ton seahorses. Every time Wednesday or Checote pushed off the bottom, they shot upward, lifting us in the air and yanking us around like we were rag dolls.

It was thrilling.
It was magical.
It was hysterical.

Once they reached deep enough water, they began to swim smoothly, pulling us behind them as we hung onto their manes, floating like river otters caught in a current. We laughed so hard we could barely function.

By the time we made it across the pond, we were completely helpless with laughter – completely soaking wet, exhausted, and happier than we'd been in ages.

That day brought us closer in a way I didn't know was possible. From then on, we proudly called ourselves the **J&S Swim Team**.

And even now, all it takes is someone saying, "Remember at Jones Forest…" and the four of us instantly lose it again.

Because that's what life is really about –
good friends, good horses, a good dog,
and one ridiculously perfect day in a Texas pond.

Swimming at Jones Forest

He Didn't Just Carry Me - Kept Me Safe

Indian George on his horse, Baby, who was from Checote's wild herd

Checote and I rode through every imaginable kind of weather on the Salt Grass Trail Ride. Over the years, we faced heartbreakingly beautiful sunrises and sunsets, gorgeous sunny days, soft misty rain, sudden thunderstorms, biting cold wind, sleet, and even snow. No matter what the sky threw at us, Checote was always steady and true. He was my best friend – the one partner I could trust with my whole life, the one horse who never gave me a single moment of fear.

There were times on that trail when I did things I probably shouldn't have. More than once, I stood straight up in the saddle just to stretch my legs or see farther ahead. And yes – I absolutely got yelled at for it. But Checote never so much as flicked an ear in irritation. He didn't stumble, didn't drift sideways, didn't speed up or slow down. He kept his pace – strong, balanced, steady as a rock – because he knew I was up there depending on him. That's who he was. A protector. A partner. A horse who understood the responsibility he carried. He was never burdened by it. It was an honor.

Checote and I were not trained cowhands – not even close – but every year we helped friends gather cattle on their ranch. When it came time to bring in the herd and separate calves for branding or doctoring, they'd ask if we could help, and we always stepped up. He wasn't a cutting horse, and I wasn't a trained cowgirl, but somehow we made it work. If I asked him to turn left, he turned. If I asked him to push a calf along, he tried. If I needed him to hold a line, he held it. He always gave me everything he had, even when the job wasn't something we normally did. Together, we figured it out. And every year, they welcomed us back because they knew that Checote's heart – and his try – were worth almost as much as any formal training.

One year, my cousin, Linda Sioux Henley, – a well-known sculptor in Texas – decided to create a bronze statue of one of our ancestors. She wanted authenticity, movement, power… and she wanted Checote and me to be her living, breathing models. I was honored. And Checote, who loved any opportunity to show off, was honored too.

I found a sewing pattern for a dress and cloak from the mid-1800s, had them made, and dressed the part. Then I hopped on Checote bareback – for a *running* photo shoot, no less – and trusted him completely. My friend, Sallie Gillispie, who is a professional and extraordinary photographer, came out to capture the moment.

We ran back and forth across that field, full-out, mane and cloak streaming behind us. Checote thundered beneath me, sure-footed and powerful, never putting a wrong foot down. Each time we turned and charged back toward Sallie, he gave the same steady, breathtaking run – ears turned toward me to listen, heart wide open, enjoying every second.

The photos were breathtaking. They looked like something pulled straight out of the past – this strong, beautiful horse carrying a woman in a billowing cloak, flying across the land. But even more incredible than the pictures was the horse beneath me.

He wasn't just a model.
He wasn't just my mount.
He was my safety, my trust, my wings.
And he proved once again that he would always, always keep me safe.

The Ride of Katy Jennings

Chapter Two - Our Lives Changed Forever

In 2005, I moved Checote and my step-sister's horse, Sister, and her mothers' horse, Coco, to a new boarding facility. It was a large property with around thirty horses sharing a thirty-acre pasture. Checote quickly found his favorite companion – a massive black draft mare named Star. I always thought it was funny how much he adored her. He was so small, and she was enormous, yet they were inseparable.

That June, tragedy struck.

Late one evening, after dark, a helicopter flew low over the pasture, its searchlight sweeping across the ground as it searched for someone. The sound and lights sent the entire herd into a panic, and they bolted to the back of the property.

Not long after the helicopter passed, the property owners decided to catch a new mare they had recently acquired and ride her in the arena, trying to take advantage of the cooler night air. (South Texas in June is unbearably hot.) As they started toward the back of the pasture, they noticed Checote and Star standing alone in the middle of the field.

What caught their attention was Star. They said she made an unbelievable maneuver - something no one could believe a horse her size could do. Then she froze, standing perfectly still, and went into what they described as a *bird dog point* position - head low, neck stretched, and one front leg lifted - pointing directly at Checote's hind leg.

It was such a strange sight that they decided to investigate. When they reached him, they immediately saw why Star had "pointed." Checote was standing, but the grass around him was crushed very close to a tree that forks, showing where he had been lying down earlier. His right hind leg had been horribly lacerated – the skin was sliced completely around the leg, all the way to the bone. The flesh had slid down several inches, exposing the entire leg bone beneath.

The owners called the vet right away, and he left immediately for the facility. Then they called me.

I don't think I've ever driven so fast in my life. I flew down the highway at a hundred miles an hour, flashers on, praying out loud the whole way. When I arrived, the vet had already stabilized Checote's leg and was trying to load him into the trailer for transport to the hospital. But Checote refused to move. He wouldn't load until I got there.

The moment I called his name and told him it was okay – that we were going to help him – he allowed the vet and my friend to help him into the trailer by helping his leg hold his weight. He trusted me completely, even in that pain.

At the hospital, Checote underwent emergency surgery to repair the leg and pulled his "sock" back up and moved the tissue back into place. When the vet finally came out, he walked straight to me and hugged me, shaking the whole time. "He made it," he said, voice thick. "He's a tough little horse." The surgery had gone well, he said – but now, it was a waiting game.

When the vet explained the extent of Checote's injuries, my heart sank. His **extensor tendons** – the ones that lift and straighten the hoof – were completely gone. The **flexor tendons**, which allow a horse the forward motion of his foot, were miraculously still intact, but the tissue surrounding them had been shredded and destroyed.

The vet told me, gently but honestly, that it was one of the worst leg injuries he had ever seen a horse survive. Without the extensor tendons, Checote would never be able to flex his foot normally again. Still, he reminded me that Checote's flexor tendons, his forward motion, was still intact, and this might give him a fighting chance – if infection could be kept at bay and if Checote had the will to recover.

Looking into Checote's eyes that night, I didn't see fear or defeat. I saw unimaginable pain, but I also saw his trust. He was calm, steady – almost reassuring *me* instead. As if to say, *We've come this far together. Don't give up on me now.*

The Long Road Back

The first weeks after the accident felt like living inside a horror film with nothing but prayer. At first, the surgeons said Checote might make a slow but full recovery. Then the prognosis slipped; one vet warned he could be "severely crippled." I drove him to Texas A&M under a sky that wouldn't make up its mind, clutching the wheel and every silent prayer I knew. The head of soft tissue surgery took his case. "He'll recover," they told me. "Sound? We can't say. Time and grace." They gave him a 50/50 chance.

Throughout it all, Checote remained consistent – cooperative, sweet, and stubborn in the ways that mattered. He hated the stall, hated the poking and prodding, but if I was there, he breathed through it. When I wasn't, he didn't. Once, while I was away, he melted down and had to be sedated – twice – just to change a bandage. When I returned, we stood in the aisle together and he let the vet touch him without a fuss, his leg shaking and his eye steady on mine. "This is a totally different horse when you are with him," the vet said. "He must trust you completely." I only smiled, because in my mind, I knew that it was a mutual complete and total trust.

By mid-July I brought him home from A&M. He couldn't back off the trailer anymore, so he turned, measured the drop, and launched – an impossible little leap for a horse with a ruined hind leg. He landed like a gymnast, eased his bad toe down, and looked around as if to say, *There. That's how we do hard things.*

His stitches didn't hold; the plan shifted to grafts once the wound was clean and ready. Meanwhile, we made a ritual of hand-walking – twice a day, slow as breath – to keep the blood moving and the hope with it. On good days his ears pricked toward the pasture, watching his friends. On the harder days, we added back a notch of painkiller and tried again tomorrow.

The wound began to granulate – tiny islands of healing that felt like miracles. He started to put weight on the leg. We fitted a toe extension so he wouldn't knuckle over at the ankle and taught his body a new geometry. Progress came unevenly: a brighter eye, a longer stride, then a day where he could barely manage the barn aisle. I learned to measure time by the smallest mercies – how far he placed his foot, whether he sighed or nickered when he saw me walking toward him.

He hated strangers near his leg. When the bandage changes with the vet became a battle, I took them over. I washed, salved, wrapped; his breathing slowed, his head lowered, and the whole ordeal softened into a quiet chore between the two of us. The A&M surgeon had said the key was sterile, regular changes. We did not miss a single one, and infection never came.

Not everything went so smoothly. When the vets were still in charge of the bandage changes, and during the leg wash, the cold hose startled him on slick concrete; he scrambled to keep from going down and clipped my shin all the way to the bone with his steel-shod hoof. Blood ran into my boot. The vet – unfazed by exposed bone on a horse – paled at the sight of mine. An urgent care visit, and a handful of stitches later, I wrapped my leg in the same green vet-wrap I used on his. We posed that night with matching bandages and ridiculous grins, the two gimps – proof that love makes fools and partners of us all. At the time, I had no idea how this event would affect Checote. He never forgot it.

Two Gimps

When the work was slow and the waiting felt long, it was the little things that kept me believing. Checote had a gentle fondness for the barn cats. He would lower his head, still wrapped in his bandages, and stand perfectly still while the cats rubbed their faces against his muzzle and slid their tails across his cheeks. Sometimes a bold little tabby would climb onto the picnic table, or even a fence rail, and stretch toward him, touching her whiskers to his face as if she were greeting an old friend.

He never pulled away. He breathed them in softly, eyes half closed, as though their small presence offered the comfort his body still couldn't find. In those quiet moments – horse and cat, I realized that his heart had never been injured at all.

Sometimes, while being hand grazed, he forgot about that leg. Instinctively, he'd shift his weight and stand on the front of his ankle, his hoof knuckled over like a folded shoe. It looked uncomfortable, almost painful, but for him it had simply become a habit – something his body did when his mind was at peace. The ligaments would softly sigh under the strain, and he would stand there, absentmindedly chewing, completely unaware that he was once again leaning on a limb that should have been protected.

I'd see it from across the small pasture, and without thinking, the words would come:
"Checote... stop that."

His ear would flick toward me. He wouldn't hurry, but he'd pause mid-chew, give a long, exaggerated sigh – and slowly, he would set the hoof flat again, placing it carefully, almost precisely, like he was reminding himself: *Right. We're still healing.*

He never argued, never fussed. It was as if he understood that I wasn't scolding him – I was protecting him. And in that quiet, oddly endearing habit, I realized just how much he trusted me... not just to lead him, but to guard him from even his own forgetfulness.

My farrier and friend, Howard Walker, came out. Before he'd seen the horse, he'd warned me I might have to face the truth of a retirement no one wanted. After watching Checote move, he stood back, blown away. "If he keeps going like this," he said, "you'll ride him again." I told him I loved him. He laughed at me and put on a clever "physical therapy" shoe that he invented and built on the spot. It had a toe extension like a rocking chair leg, and it was effective in stopping his ankle from folding under him.

We had tried turnouts in a tiny arena. At first, without me at his shoulder, he forgot to think about his steps and dropped onto the front of his ankle. We pulled him out. Two weeks later, with the new shoe and more practice, he negotiated ruts and uneven ground without a single misstep. Then he did what Checote always did: he celebrated. Head high, tail flagged, a tiny buck of joy – and he came down on the bad leg. He shook it off, but the message stuck. No more unsupervised romps; we would temper our victories with caution.

By September, Hurricane Rita was spinning toward the coast. I was working in Norway and flew home early to evacuate. The trip north was long and hot, the air thick with fear. He stepped off the trailer in Fort Worth on three legs, exhausted but still proud. When we returned days later, he was stiff again, and I could've cried from guilt. I hosed his leg and whispered apologies into his mane. "You don't argue with a hurricane, boy," I said. "You just get out of its way." He forgave me in the only currency that matters between a horse and a woman: he let me lift his leg and wrap it again.

In October and November, another surgery at A&M helped the wound turn a corner. It stopped hurting to the touch. His control over the hoof improved; he could step up, load, and negotiate inclines like a horse who'd been practicing patience as a discipline. He'd steal a half-buck at the end of the lead rope when an invented "horse-eating monster" passed – always just a shadow at the edge of his eye, always just enough to remind us that his heart was still wild.

By Christmas, a new worry crowded the hope. His gait grew jerky – high-stepping with the injured leg and flopping the foot down like a puppet whose strings were pulled too hard. Concrete was the worst; he hesitated, braced, sometimes refused. The vets named it: stringhalt, a nerve problem, the last remaining tendon overstimulated and working too much, too fast. The recommended fix was to sever that tendon. I knew the literature; I knew they weren't wrong. I also knew I couldn't ask him to give up the last thing holding that hoof in line.

Instead, we turned to motion and friendship. I asked to turn him out in a small pen during the day with Coco as his companion. They agreed. It worked. Week by week, the exaggerated lift softened on grass and arena dirt; hard ground still showed the hitch, but even there, he improved. I began ponying him from Coco down quiet trails – just a little, just enough to remind his body how to be a horse and his spirit how to be free. During Rachael's barrel lessons, he'd stand at the fence and nicker when she loped past, a one-horse cheering section in a blanket and rehab shoe.

The barn remained the same: a place where sorrows and small miracles shared a tack room. One afternoon, my step-father, Jack, set a barn cat on Checote's blanketed back and led them for a turn around the arena. The cat rode like a prince. Checote flicked an ear, pleased to be trusted. No one had sat on his back in months; it counted.

By late January, even the vets are smiling when they watch him move. His steps are lighter now, almost buoyed by something unseen.
"End of February," they say. "Possibly early March. You could be riding him in the arena."

I don't just hear them. This time, I believe them.

In my heart, I feel it already – the quiet lift of his withers as he carries me, the warmth of his breath, the rhythm that once taught me trust:
steady… steady… steady.

It doesn't feel like just a recovery anymore. It feels like a promise.

I don't pretend I never doubted. I worried about money, about travel, about being the only person he let near his leg. I worried that his love of speed would outpace his healing. I worried because that's what you do when your heart lives outside your body with four hooves and a will of his own. But twice per week, I re-wrapped the wound. Every morning, he set his foot down a hair more surely than the day before. Friends prayed. Doctors cut and stitched. Howard hammered and rasped. And Checote – my fierce, opinionated, gentle, miraculous horse – kept choosing forward.

"Will he ever ride Salt Grass again?" people asked. I didn't know. Maybe 2007, we said, half joke, half vow. What I did know was this: the road back was long, and we were already on it – two souls moving as one, learning all over again how to fly without ever leaving the ground.

Learning to Fly Again

Coco and Checote

I moved Checote and Coco to the new barn for a simple reason: it was closer to both my office and my home, cutting precious minutes from the drive and giving me more time where I most needed it – with him. By then we had officially retired Sister, my step-sister Rachael's beloved mare, and Rachael had taken over riding Coco. So, it was just these two horses who made the trip to Callegari, and honestly, that suited Checote just fine. Coco had become his steady companion, his soft place to land. And after all he'd survived, familiarity mattered.

The boarding facility, **Callegari**, met us with open arms and practical kindness. They *listened* when I explained Checote's special needs and offered any help they could. They let me set up a small, temporary pen so Checote could have limited turnout with Coco as his only companion.

Coco understood him in a way only another horse could – stepping gently near his injured leg, steadying herself whenever he needed calm. Compassion takes a different shape in a horse, but you recognize it the moment you see it. Coco was one of Checote's guardian angels on this earth. She watched over him, warned me when something was wrong, and protected him with the quiet strength only she possessed.

At first, our rides didn't involve riding at all – at least not with me in the saddle.

Instead, I introduced **cavaletti work**: simple raised poles spaced evenly across the ground. It sounds small – stepping over poles – but for a horse with a missing extensor tendon, it was physical therapy, brain therapy, and hope therapy all in one.

The first day, I walked him over the poles by hand. He had to think about every footfall, every lift and placement of his injured hoof. He worked hard. I could see his concentration in the line of his neck, the flick of his ears. And every time he cleared a pole without knuckling over, I felt a spark of triumph.

Eventually, we raised the poles an inch at a time. Then we trotted them – carefully, evenly – teaching his legs a new language.
A softer one.
A deliberate one.

When he grew strong enough, I saddled him – not to ride him, just to let him carry the weight and remember the feel of purpose. He lifted his head, ears bright, as if proud to wear the saddle again. Like he was saying, *I'm still a horse. I still have a job.*

From there, the real magic happened.

Practicing the Trails

I began riding Coco on the trail and ponying Checote beside us. At first, we walked slow, steady steps. The three of us in a quiet line through the dappled woods. Then, little by little, Checote asked for more.

I felt it before I saw it – the coil of energy, the eagerness in his stride.

One morning, with dew glistening on the grass, he shifted from walk to trot beside Coco, smooth and balanced. Weeks later, he asked for a canter, and I let him. He moved beautifully, ears pricked, tail lifted, carrying the saddle weight like it was nothing.

Then came the day he galloped beside her – truly galloped – and for a heartbeat I saw the horse he had been before the accident.

My heart swelled.

He wasn't healed completely. But he was healing.

And Carry Me He Did

First Ride After the Accident

I'll never forget the day he was ready.

There was no announcement, no grand sign – just a feeling deep in my chest, the same feeling you get when you finally know a wound has closed, even before you look.

I tightened the girth, placed my foot in the stirrup, and eased onto his back. He stood perfectly still, ears flicked back toward me, waiting. When I settled into the saddle, we both exhaled – the same long breath – and everything inside me clicked into place.

We began in the arena, walking slow, deliberate circles. He moved carefully at first, as if remembering each piece of the job. I kept my hand light, letting him know he could set the pace. We didn't rush a thing.

But something in him was awakening – a spark, a memory, a desire.

After a few days, we ventured onto the trails, with Coco beside us. She came along just in case he needed a break. The leaves whispered overhead, the sun broke through the branches, and Checote walked with growing confidence. The trails had always been our sanctuary, and he remembered them like an old song.

Then came the moment we'd both been waiting for.

He asked for a trot.

He lifted into it without hesitation – smooth, rhythmic, eager. I could feel the joy radiating from him. He tossed his head once, not in pain, but in happiness.

A few rides later, he asked for a canter.

His stride lengthened beneath me, his body flowing like water over stone. I laughed – I couldn't help it – and he flicked an ear back at me as if to say, *See? I told you I could.*

And finally, months after the accident that was supposed to end everything, we added speed.

Not recklessly, not wildly – but gloriously.

He ran.

Not as fast as before, not as freely perhaps – but he ran with heart. With power. With pride. He ran because he wanted to.

He could do it.

And he did.

In that moment, I felt everything – the fear, the pain, the months of doubt and sleeplessness – melt into the wind. All that remained was the truth:

My little horse, who was never supposed to run again, was flying.

And this time, I let myself fly with him.

Riding Checote with Coco

The Play Day

I arrived at the barn one Saturday, not terribly long after I had begun riding Checote on the trails again. I was looking forward to spending the day trail riding with Sallie and Rachael. Instead, I found the barn crowded with people, horses, and nonstop activity.

Callegari was hosting a Play Day.

I had never seen one before, much less competed in one. I simply don't have a competitive bone in my body. Sallie and Rachael were interested in participating, so I agreed to that instead of our planned trail ride.

There were several different events happening throughout the day, some with multiple classes divided by age groups. I had never even seen most of these events, so I had absolutely no idea what I was doing. Sallie described them to me, and I decided that Checote and I would enter Western Pleasure in the 18-and-over class, the Obstacle Course, and a Team Western Pleasure with Rachael.

Now, I had never even *seen* a Western Pleasure class before, much less competed in one. Sallie explained that you simply ride around the perimeter of the arena while the announcer calls out gait changes. I thought, *How hard can that be?*

Well… it wasn't exactly easy for a horse without an extensor tendon who was still learning his new way of moving.

Each time a gait was called and I asked Checote for the transition, he listened and responded — as smoothly as a handicapped horse could. He tried every single time. In the end, Checote was awarded fourth place. Which really wasn't bad for a class of over 20 participants.

I didn't care about the placing. What mattered to me was that he impressed the judges with his willingness, his calm demeanor, and the amount of try he showed despite everything his body had been through.

Next came the Obstacle Course. Once again, I thought, *How hard can it be?*

For a seasoned trail horse, most of it wasn't — until we reached the portion that required backing a straight line at quite a distance between poles and then executing a ninety-degree turn. *That* was hard for a horse with missing extensor tendons.

Backing up frustrated Checote. We stopped, regrouped, and tried again. He never crossed the poles he was meant to stay inside. Though he was slow, he completed the challenge successfully, and was awarded third place.

The final event was Team Western Pleasure. Rachael and Coco were our teammates. In this class, you were required to hold hands with your partner while transitioning through the called gaits without breaking the handhold. The last pair to break handhold were the winner.

This part was a breeze.

Checote and Coco were already accustomed to staying in sync on the trail, and Rachael and I followed their lead easily. We took home the blue ribbon.

We celebrated with a victory lap around the arena, galloping fast with our hands held high in the air.

For a small horse recovering from such a devastating injury, that victory lap meant far more to us than winning any ribbon. I could feel the pride rising from Checote, and I know he could feel just how proud I was of him too.

Healing isn't just survival — it's participation, trust, and joy returning.

Creature Comforts

It's funny the things you learn about a horse when you've spent years together – not the big things, but the small, quiet preferences that reveal who they are at their core.

Checote had opinions.
Strong ones.

And he was never shy about letting me know about the ones that mattered to him the most.

The Night Checote Set Himself on Fire

Checote hated to be cold.
I don't mean he disliked it – I mean he *hated* it. The kind of deep, dramatic, personal hatred that makes a horse behave like the world is ending if a chilly breeze dares to brush his royal hide. He could handle heat, rain, mud, or sleet, but cold? That was his sworn enemy.

One year on the Salt Grass Trail Ride, before his accident, we were packed into Katy Park like sardines. Horse trailers lined up in rows so tight you could knock on your neighbor's window without leaving the doorway of your rig. It was a bitterly cold night, the kind where the air stings your nose and the wind sneaks under every layer of clothing you own.

I'd blanketed Checote, of course, tucking him in like the oversized, dramatic toddler he was. But apparently, that still wasn't warm enough for His Highness.

At some point in the night, he decided to take matters into his own hooves.

Trying to warm himself up, he shuffled over and pressed his blanketed side against the heat exhaust of the travel trailer parked right next to us.

Yes.
The heat exhaust.

Within moments – poof – his blanket caught fire.

Thankfully, a passerby saw smoke curling up from the side of my horse. They reacted fast, and disaster was avoided, but not before the damage was done. The fire burned a clean, round hole straight through his blanket and singed a neat patch of hair right off his side.

When I got to him, Checote wasn't acting tender, stressed, or dramatic in the slightest. Honestly, he seemed more embarrassed than anything – as if he knew he'd done something ridiculous and hoped nobody would tell the other horses.

I had a friend rush over with burn salve, and we treated the spot immediately. He healed just fine – but the legend only grew after that.

To this day, I still say:
I am the only person I know whose horse managed to accidentally set himself on fire.

But that was Checote – determined, intelligent, stubborn, dramatic, and always trying to solve life's problems on his own terms. Even if that meant nearly turning himself into a campfire.

Checote Wants Warm Water When The Weather is Cold

Tammy, Coco & Checote Freezing on the SGTR

Callegari was a beautiful boarding facility – clean, organized, and so well-run it felt like a luxury resort for horses. Every stall had automatic waterers, which most horses thought were wonderful. But it didn't take me long to learn that Checote did *not* share their enthusiasm… especially on cold nights.

The water that trickled into those bowls was icy, the kind that made your teeth ache just thinking about it. In the summer, the cold water is what you would want. But Checote didn't like it during cold weather. Checote would walk over, wrinkle his nose, take one offended sniff, and turn his head away with dramatic flair – as if the very idea of drinking cold water in cold weather was beneath him.

So every chilly evening, I'd hang a bucket of warm water in his stall. He'd drink it down gratefully, then raise his head and look at me with those soft eyes that said, *That was lovely… perhaps just*

one more?
And of course, I'd refill it before I left for the night.

His dislike of cold water wasn't new. Even on the Salt Grass Trail Ride – which takes place in February – I'd end up warming his drinking water on the RV stove just so he would hydrate. We jokingly called it *"Checote's Tea."* Riders around us would laugh, and I'd wave them off, saying, "Oh, he's not spoiled at all!"

But between us – me and that horse – we both knew better.

He was absolutely spoiled…
and he had earned every bit of it.

The Saddle Spoke - And Checote Agreed

The saddle I had used on Checote for years finally gave out. I sent it off to be repaired, but after the sheepskin was replaced nothing about it fit the same. No matter what girth I used or how I padded it, the girth rubbed him raw. Although he was clear to me in his dislike of the saddle after the sheepskin replacement, he tolerated it because he trusted me, and was patient as I tried different girths and pads to try to correct it. But the moment I saw the sores forming, that was it.

I started saving for the saddle I knew would suit him best – a *Circle Y Flex-Lite*. Until I could afford it, we went back to basics. We rode bareback or with a simple pad. It didn't matter to us; we were together, and that was enough. Honestly, bareback riding made us feel like we were one creature with a shared heartbeat, and he always seemed to lift me a little higher, more carefully, as if saying, *Don't worry, I've got you.*

And he always did.

Lia

Lia on her horse, Regent

Checote was still fiercely protective of his injured leg. For months, I was the only one he would allow to come near it – let alone touch it – to change the bandages. But life doesn't stand still, even for healing horses. I still had to work, and my job often required me to travel overseas – often for a week at a time.
So what was I supposed to do?

There was a young high-school girl at the barn, Lia – gentle, kind, and soft-spoken. And to make things even sweeter, Checote adored her. I often did his bandage changes while he stood untied at the hitching post, calm and relaxed. That is, unless Lia walked by. Then all bets were off. He would leave the post without hesitation, following her with bright eyes and perked ears, doing everything short of tapping her on the shoulder to demand her attention – and all the pets he believed he was entitled to.

I asked her if she would be willing to take over his bandage changes while I was away. She lit up – honored to help and happy to earn a little extra money. I taught her how to clean the wound, pad it, wrap it, and secure it just right. Too loose, and it would fall off. Too tight, and it could cut off circulation and jeopardize the healing of that precious leg.

She listened carefully. And then – she did it perfectly. Every. Single. Time.

But it wasn't just her careful hands that helped him heal.
It was the tenderness.
The patience.
The connection.

It was the way she talked to him softly while she worked, telling him he was a good boy, thanking him for trusting her.

Lia didn't just change his bandages.
She cared for his spirit, too.

And that – more than any ointment, medicine, or wrap – is an essential part of healing.

Another Setback

Then came the day I noticed something new – a hesitation.

Checote began balking whenever we approached the concrete walkway in the barn. If I was in the saddle, he walked across without a second thought. But if I was leading him on foot, he'd stop at the edge, lower his head, and sniff the ground as if studying it. Then, carefully, he would lift his injured leg and hop across on three legs, refusing to let that hoof touch the hard surface.

If he did lower his foot, the stringhalt – that sudden, jerky motion that had haunted him for months – would return instantly. But the moment we stepped back onto dirt, it vanished again, as if the earth itself offered him comfort.

When he stopped to smell the ground, I was always patient with him. I never hurried him or tugged at the lead rope. I simply waited – letting him take all the time he needed to figure it out for himself. I'd learned long ago that Checote responded best to trust, not pressure. Eventually, he'd take a breath, lift his head, and step forward, knowing I'd be right there beside him.

The hesitation on concrete worried me enough to call the vet. After her exam, the diagnosis stunned me: pain. She believed the hard surface was sending "stingers" up his leg. Her plan was straightforward – start pain management medication and ask my farrier to fit rubber shoes.

So I called Howard.

His response was pure Howard. "He's not in pain," he said flatly. "He's cautious. Without extensor tendons, that leg doesn't land the way it used to. He flops the foot down and slides it into place – and he's afraid of slipping." Rubber, he warned, would make matters worse. His fix was simple: borium nails for grip so the foot wouldn't skate out from under him on slick concrete.

I was torn. In my gut, Howard's explanation fit what I'd been seeing. But if the vet was right and Checote *was* hurting, I couldn't miss it. I needed clarity – one more way to listen to my horse.

That's when I had an idea: call **Sonya Fitzpatrick**. If anyone could help me understand what Checote was feeling, it was her.

Chapter Three – Learning to Hear What Is Not Spoken

Sonya Fitzpatrick

Sonja Fitzpatrick

I'd first seen Sonya years earlier on her show, *The Pet Psychic* on the *Discovery Channel*. She had been working with a woman whose horse had inexplicably stopped loading into their trailer. What caught my attention was that the horse loaded perfectly for strangers – just not the owner.

Within minutes, Sonya uncovered the problem. She told the woman, "You're allergic to wasp and bee stings." Sure enough, there was a wasp nest hidden inside the trailer. They knocked it down, and from that moment on, the horse loaded perfectly – no fear, no hesitation.

That story had stuck with me. Sonya didn't just read animals – She seemed to be someone who could understand not just animals, but the bond between animals and their people – that was someone I needed now.

I scheduled an appointment at Sonya's first available opening. Her website made the process easy, and it asked for a photo of each animal. I uploaded a picture of Checote taken long before his accident – his brown and white coat glowing, his eyes bright and proud. Since you were allowed to add up to three animals, I also uploaded photos of my two dogs, Tanner and Madison.

What followed was one of the most extraordinary conversations of my life.

When the time for my appointment with Sonya Fitzpatrick finally arrived, I sat in my office with the phone pressed to my ear and my heart beating like I was waiting for a doctor to deliver life-changing news. I'd watched this woman talk to animals through a television screen, watched her reach into the space between species and pull out truth after truth with uncanny clarity.
Now it was my turn.

I didn't know if she would be vague or specific, comforting or strange, accurate or wildly off the mark. All I knew was that I needed one thing: clarity.
Clarity about pain.
Fear.
Healing.
And most of all, about my horse.

Her voice came through gentle and warm, touched with that soft English lilt I recognized immediately.

"Hello, Tammy. I've been looking at your animals."

A laugh escaped me. "Oh good!"

She chuckled softly, as though she could feel the swirl of my emotions. "Let's begin, shall we?"

But the first name she spoke wasn't Checote.

It was Leah.

Leah

Leah & Tammy napping at the lunch break on the Salt Grass Trail Ride

Almost as soon as our session began, Sonya said softly, "You have another horse – not just the one in the picture you sent me."

I was stunned. "Yes," I said, "her name is Leah."

"She isn't with Checote," Sonya continued. "Where is she now?"

I explained that Leah lived on a friend's parents' ranch in New Waverly, Texas. Sonya nodded. "She likes it there. She doesn't want to leave. She says she's retired now – she repeats that word, *retired*."

I smiled. "Yes, she is. She earned it."

Sonya paused, listening to something I couldn't hear. "What happened to her left leg? It started with pain in her left leg, but her right leg hurts more than the left now. It's in her joints."

That took me aback. Leah had broken her *left* stifle as a young horse. "She's probably been compensating all these years," I said quietly. "It would make sense that the right leg hurts now."

"She's afraid of the pain," Sonya said gently, as though speaking to Leah directly. "It's alright to be afraid. Sometimes legs just hurt."

Sonya went on to describe the woman who cared for Leah. "Leah says that woman thinks like a horse," Sonya said, smiling. "She loves her dearly."

Then she added something unexpected. "Leah would like her blue halter back."

I frowned. "She's never had a blue halter."

Sonya laughed softly. "Well, she says she did."

Then it hit me. Years ago, when Leah was being used as a broodmare, my friend, Kenny, who bred her had put a blue halter on her after her first foal was born. It wasn't mine – it had belonged to him – but I still had a photo of her wearing it pinned to my bulletin board.

"If she can't have *that* one," Sonya said, "she'd like another blue halter instead."

"I'll get her one," I promised.

Sonya smiled. "Bring it when you visit her – with the apple treats. She says those are her favorite."

Madison and Tanner

Madison & Tanner

Next came my dogs. Sonya immediately focused on **Madison**, my chocolate Lab. "One of the dogs had a previous owner," she said. "She was tied up most of the time, couldn't move far, and often wasn't fed enough."

That sounded right. "Madison came from the SPCA," I told her. "I don't know her full story."

"She was grateful to be there," Sonya said. "They fed her regularly, and she was safe for the first time. But she never imagined life could be *this* good. She loves you. She loves her home. She can't believe her luck."

Then Sonya smiled. "Who owns the sparkly brownish car? Madison loves that car."

I laughed. "That's my husband's SUV – hard to describe color, kind of metallic."

"She says it's the most beautiful car she's ever seen. But, she doesn't ride in that one. She rides in the other car with the beige seat – that's hers, you know." I confirmed that Madison only rode in my truck with beige interior and the seat folded flat. I always laid it down when the dogs went with me anywhere.

Then we talked about **Tanner**, my German Shepherd–Husky mix. "He's full of himself," Sonya said with a grin. "But he adores you. He says you kiss him a lot – and he loves it."

She described his playful relationship with Madison, his love of chicken and hamburgers, and even mentioned his surgery. "There was something on his chest that caused him pain," she said. "It's gone now, and he feels much better.". Yes, we had a tumor surgically removed from his chest. Sonya confirmed that it needed to be removed, as it restricted his breathing.

Checote

Finally, I asked, "What about Checote?"

There was a long pause. Then Sonya said softly, "You ride this horse. He likes it when you ride him. Do you know how much he loves you?"

"Yes," I said, "I love him the same."

"No," she said gently. "I mean, he *really* loves you. He adores you. He never wants anyone else to own him, because no one understands him like you do."

I smiled. "I love him just as much."

Sonya seemed to be listening for a moment, then said, "Checote likes it when you breathe in his nostrils. He likes to share the air with you." I replied, "Yes, he sure does. He puts his muzzle in my face or on my head all the time."

Sonya laughed suddenly. "He says he's the most beautiful horse in the whole barn! He loves to toss his head high when he runs – he says he's a *good head tosser.*"

That was pure Checote.

Sonya asked, "When did you move him?" I replied, "16 months ago." Sonya said, "Checote wants to know if we are staying here? They are good to him at this place." I replied that I was super happy to know that they are good to Checote at this barn, and that for our foreseeable future, the plan was to stay.

Sonya paused again, listening. "He says the old saddle hurt his back. The new one feels good. He only wants you to use that one from now on."

I nodded, surprised. "I just replaced his saddle a few months ago," I said. "The old one started galling him."

Then Sonya smiled again. "He's very grateful for his new bucket."

I laughed. "New bucket? I didn't buy one." Then I realized what she meant – the warm water bucket that I'd been hanging each night because he hated the automatic waterer.

"That's it," she said. "He appreciates it very much."

What Happened That Night

When I asked about his **accident**, Sonya's tone changed. "He's running. Everyone is running. His leg was caught and couldn't get free," she said softly. "He panicked because there was so much pain. He's very careful now – he never wants to be hurt like that again."

I asked the question that had haunted me: "Does it hurt when I ride him?"

"Sometimes," she said honestly. "He needs more time. The pain comes and goes."

"Does it hurt when he walks on the concrete?" I asked.

She shook her head. "No pain – fear. He's afraid of slipping and hurting you. He stops to look because he needs to be sure it's safe. You wait for him, and he knows that. He appreciates your patience."

Then she added, "His biggest fear isn't falling – it's *you* getting hurt. He's careful because he never wants you to be hurt."

That nearly broke me. I knew it was true. He had fallen not long after his accident, and I got hurt. We wore matching bandages on the same leg.

Sonja asked, who was the young girl that occasionally rode him. "He likes her, but she's too bossy. She wants to look perfect, and he can feel that. He says he only wants *your* seat on his back." She laughed. "His exact words were, *'I only want her ass on my back!'*"

I burst out laughing. That was my boy!

Sonya went on to describe his love for warmth, the way he appreciated his leg wrap – because he *hates* it when his leg is cold, actually, she said he *hates* to be cold at all – and his excitement about the new turnout area being built for him and Coco. She told me he wanted to know *when* it would be finished so he could look forward to it.

"He'll wait," she said, smiling. "Just tell him when it's coming."

When the session ended, I sat quietly for a long time, my heart full. Whether or not anyone else would believe it didn't matter to me. Sonya had put words to things I had *felt* for years – I knew what resonated. Checote's protectiveness, his pride, his humor, his deep and loyal love.

Everything she said about my horse – my sweet, proud, loving Checote – rang like truth.

As I hung up the phone, I whispered into the quiet room, "I hear you, Cote. I hear you."

For the first time since the accident, I felt like I truly understood what he needed – not just physically, but spiritually.

And that changed everything.

And as strange as it might sound, after that day, I felt even closer to him. It was as if the things we'd always understood in silence had finally been spoken aloud.

Enter Lindsey

As the months passed, Checote continued to improve – stronger, surer, and more himself with each week. My step-sister eventually gave up horseback riding, and I officially became Coco's owner as well. I had always been her caretaker, so life for Coco didn't change too much. She always thought she belonged to me anyway.

Life at the barn had its own rhythm. Horses came and went, boarders moved in and out, friendships formed quickly over grooming stalls and trail rides. But every so often, someone arrived who shifted the entire energy of a place.

That someone was Lindsey.

I didn't know anything about her at first – just that she was sweet and rode a handsome gray horse named Jack. I liked them both. Rumor spread quickly that she was an *animal communicator*, but barns collect rumors the way horses collect burrs, so it kind of went in one ear and out the other.

Every Saturday a group of us rode together, and that's how I got to know Lindsey a little better. She was friendly and easy to talk to. One afternoon after our ride, I was hand-grazing Checote and Coco when Lindsey wandered over to chat. As we talked, she asked casually, "How did Checote hurt his leg?"

I told her I didn't know for sure – only that the owners of the property where he was injured had found him that night. Lindsey grew quiet for a moment, then said softly, "He's showing me what happened."

She described what Checote was "saying": He was running. All the horses were running. He ran through the middle of a broken tree. His leg got caught, and he couldn't get free. He fell. There was so much pain, Tammy. Just so much pain!

My breath left my body in a shudder.

Because that – *that* – made sense.

I told her that when they found him, he had been beside a tree that forked close to the ground. The barn owners had always assumed he'd been lying down there and had startled when the helicopter flew over, accidentally jamming his leg into the fork as he scrambled up. That explanation had never quite made sense to me. But Lindsey's description did.

I hesitated, then asked, "Does Checote know who saved his life that night?"

Lindsey's brow furrowed. "He keeps talking about *the other horse,*" she said slowly. "But I see a lot of horses in that pasture."

"He means Star," I told her. "She was his girlfriend – a big black draft mare."

At that, Lindsey froze. Even though the day was sweltering, goosebumps rose along her arms.

"What's wrong?" I asked.

"I'm not sure if I should tell you," she said quietly. "I don't know what your belief system is."

"You can't stop there," I said. "Just tell me."

Lindsey took a breath. "Checote said there were *two angels* in the pasture that night. They told the other horse what to do – how to get him help."

Now it was my turn to get goosebumps. Suddenly, Star's strange behavior that night – the "bird-dog point," the way she drew the owners' attention to Checote – made perfect, impossible sense.

Two angels.

Star "pointing" to his leg.
Star behaving in ways that made *no sense* for a horse her size.
The owners stopping – inexplicably – because of her behavior.

Suddenly, it all fit.

I felt the world shift under my feet – a small shift, but enough that I knew life had just divided into *before* and *after*. Before Lindsey… and now, after.

We stood there for a long moment, the breeze stirring the grass, my horses tugging at the grass, while Lindsey continued speaking in that soft, steady voice that was always laced with laughter.

"He says he used to run all the time," she said. "That he loved it. That he felt… free."

I smiled sadly. "He did. Before the accident he was a runner."

"He liked to race the wind," she added. "And… he says he used to toss his head when he was happy."

I laughed – the sound surprising me. "He still does."

She continued describing his personality before I ever met him – things I had only known from stories told by Tom or Indian George. Things I'd felt from him instinctively. Things no one at this barn had ever heard.

She shouldn't have known any of it. But she did. Everything she said rang true.

Then she turned to Coco.

"She's thirsty," she said suddenly.

I blinked. "She is?"

"She's telling me she wants water."

We walked to the stock tank, Coco stepping faster with each stride.

Sure enough, she plunged her nose straight into the water and drank deeply. I just stared, stunned, because every horse owner knows, you can lead a horse to water, but you can't make them drink.

"She's had two babies," Lindsey added.

My mouth fell open. "I don't know her history."

Later, when I contacted her former owner, every detail was confirmed. Coco had indeed had two foals – one a champion roping horse.

Lindsey wasn't guessing. She wasn't guessing at all.

Before we parted that day, Lindsey told me more about herself – how she had refined her gift for animal communication through meditation, and how she could also work with energy to help animals heal. I listened with interest and tucked that bit of information away.

Little did I know then just how much Lindsey – and her quiet, remarkable gift – would help me and my animals in the years to come.

Lindsey & Jack

Chapter Four – The Miracles Begin

Lindsey Helps Checote Walk On Concrete

Not long after Lindsey's original conversation with Checote, I asked if she could check in with him again to see if she could add anything to what Sonya had received about his difficulty walking on concrete. He had definitely shown improvement after Howard put borium nails on his hind shoes – especially when I walked beside him. The hesitation had almost vanished, and even the stringhalt had eased some, although it didn't disappear completely. Some days were better than others.

So, we scheduled a session at the barn.

Lindsey knew immediately that there was interference in Checote's leg that was causing the stringhalt. Yes, there was nerve pain – those little "stingers" that would fire now and then – but that wasn't the whole issue, or even much of an issue. He no longer felt safe walking on concrete, even with the borium nails that gave him extra grip. He had lost some feeling in that foot. And because concrete doesn't conduct energy like the earth does, he couldn't interpret where his hoof was in relation to the ground. The sensory feedback – the natural grounding that horses rely on – simply wasn't there. His proprioception had faded, leaving him unsure, guarded, and hesitant.

Lindsey had me walk him down the long concrete aisle of the barn while she observed him from behind. His steps were uncertain, careful, almost questioning. When we reached the far end, we turned and walked back toward her.

When we approached, Lindsey simply lowered her hands toward the bandaged leg and gently laid them there.

What stunned me was that Checote didn't try to kick her.

He had been fiercely protective of that injured leg. He had warned off so many others with quick, sharp pot shots if they reached for it without permission. But this time, he didn't resist. He didn't even tense.

What I didn't know then – but learned later – was that before she ever touched him, Lindsey quietly asked for his permission. She promised she would do nothing to harm him, nothing to bring pain, and nothing to set him back.

He believed her.

After a few quiet minutes, Lindsey asked me to walk him down the barn aisle again.

This time – there was no stringhalt.

Not a trace.

His stride was smooth. Confident. Balanced. He knew where his foot was. He trusted the ground beneath him again.

And incredibly, it stayed gone – not just for days or weeks,
but for **years**.

It didn't return until Checote's brave and faithful body had finally had enough and was ready to rest.

Lindsey Helps Madison

Tammy's house where the incident happened

It was the summer of 2007. I got home around 10 p.m. after a long day – work, the barn, then a grocery run. My arms were full of grocery bags when I opened the front door, and before I could even step inside, Tanner (my Husky–Shepherd mix) and Madison (my Chocolate Lab) darted out, nearly knocking me over.

They ran into the empty lot next door, noses down, tails up. I halfheartedly called after them, but they ignored me completely. Setting the groceries down on the kitchen counter, I went back outside and called again – this time with my *"you'd better listen to me"* voice.

They both came flying toward me, Tanner first, bounding through the grass. Madison, who was closer to the street, veered toward the road instead of the yard. Maybe she thought the pavement would be easier to run on. She never saw – or heard – the car coming.

The impact made a sound I'll never forget. I screamed her name, but it was too late. The car hit her in the left hip, slamming her onto the pavement. I watched it happen and could do nothing to stop it. The driver never slowed down, never looked back, he never saw her.

Madison was lying twisted on the pavement, screaming in pure agony. But somehow, impossibly, she got up. Her scream tore through me. I shouted her name and sprinted toward her, heart pounding so hard I could feel it in my teeth. Somehow she started trying to run toward me – her leg just dangling, her body twisted, still screaming. Her back left leg dangled uselessly behind her as she limped toward me, her whole body shaking with pain. I knelt down as we reached each other, and tried to calm her. There was no blood, but her leg looked wrong. Very wrong.

I laid the backseat of my truck down to make a flat surface and loaded her in as gently as I could.

I called the Animal Emergency Room on the way, telling them I was coming in with a dog that had been hit by a car.

Then I called my husband.

And lastly, I called Lindsey.

Her voicemail answered.

"Lindsey, it's Tammy," I said in what I'm sure was a panicked voice. "My dog's been hit by a car. Please call me."

She called back less than a minute later. "Tammy," she said, her voice calm but certain, "her back left leg and hip took the blow. Nothing's broken. Her hip was out of place in two spots, and her leg in one. I've moved them back. She has bruises and contusions all down her hip and leg, but I've healed everything I could find. If she's stiff or sore tomorrow, call me and I'll do more."

I hadn't even told her *which dog* was hurt. How did she know it was the female?

By then, I'd reached the emergency vet. When I opened the back door of my truck, Madison leaped out like nothing had happened – tail wagging, full of life, pulling me straight toward the clinic door. Madison never just *walked* on a leash; she towed me. She wiggled her whole backside in excitement, waiting for me to open the door.

The receptionist looked over the counter and blinked at the sight of this happy, wriggling dog. "Are you sure she was hit by a car?" she asked.

"Yes," I said, probably a bit too loudly. "I saw it happen. I heard it happen. She was slammed to the ground, she was screaming. I'm *positive* she was hit by a car."

The vet examined her from head to tail, palpating along her sides, hips, and legs. "Nothing's broken," she said, frowning. "No swelling, no tenderness, there's not even a bruise that I can find."

Again: "Are you sure she was hit by a car?"

I could hardly believe what I was hearing. I demanded x-rays.

Two full-body x-rays later, the results came back: nothing broken, nothing dislocated. The only thing the vet found was arthritis – both hips full of it. Hardly a surprise for a twelve-year-old Lab.

Madison walked out of that clinic like nothing had ever happened. She wagged her tail, pulled me toward the truck, and jumped right in.

That night, I sat beside her and thought about the phone call, about how Lindsey somehow knew exactly which dog, which leg, which hip, even the number of joints affected. I couldn't explain it, but I didn't need to.

That was Madison's miracle.

Meeting Lindsey was not an accident.

And neither, I suspected, was anything that was about to unfold.

Madison sleeping behind the couch after she was hit

Checote's Infected Leg

The scar on Checote's hind leg had always been a fragile thing – a tight ring of scar tissue wrapped around the bone like a reminder of the night he almost died. No hair grew there. It bruised easily. It healed slowly. I had learned long ago that this patch of skin didn't behave like normal skin; it was more like thin parchment stretched over a wound the body never fully forgot. His missing extensor tendons – the two that lift the front of the hoof – give him a faintly unusual gait, but by now most people never notice.

Since it had always been vulnerable, and when a small sore opened in the center of that scar again, I wasn't surprised. I'd managed spots like it before – gentle cleaning, careful wrapping, patience. But this one was darker, larger, edged in blackish purple. Something about it unsettled me. I made an appointment at the Texas A&M Large Animal Veterinary Hospital, where Checote was already a private patient of Dr. Rakestraw, the head of the Soft Tissue Injury Department.

But Checote didn't wait for that appointment. On a Sunday evening, everything changed.

I arrived at the barn for my usual visit and immediately knew something was very wrong. When I led Checote from his stall, I froze. His injured leg was grotesquely swollen from hock to fetlock, hot with fever. The small sore was oozing yellow pus. The infection was unmistakable – and terrifying.

The infection wasn't mild. It was raging.

"Cote," I whispered, my voice thin and shaking. "Oh Boy… what happened?"

He looked at me with those deep, liquid eyes – hurting, but trusting. Always trusting.

I led him from his stall, and the moment he stepped into the aisle, Coco – his constant companion – leaned over her stall door, ears pinned forward, watching every movement. She sensed something was wrong. Horses always know.

I pulled Coco out and tied her nearby to keep him calm. Then I crouched beside his leg, and gently ran cool water over the swollen flesh trying to cool the fever. The heat rising off it was alarming. Since scar tissue doesn't stretch like normal skin; it looked as if the swelling could tear it open at any moment.

I was afraid infection had entered his bloodstream. His eyes told me he didn't feel well. As I called A&M to tell them I was bringing him in, I continued to run cool water over his leg. Coco stood watching closely, lowering her face to his leg, looking from the wound to me as if she knew something wasn't right and was begging me to *Do Something*.

Two friends at the barn came running when they saw the swelling. They helped me hitch the trailer and load Checote as quickly as possible. Before loading him, I wrapped his leg loosely in a soft polo wrap, careful not to add pressure to the already swollen tissue. The scar tissue doesn't stretch – it's not like normal skin – and I was afraid too much tension would make it split open.

By then, I'd been caring for Checote's leg for over three years. I didn't panic easily anymore. Nothing short of death would ever equal the fear of his original injury. I knew when something was serious – and this was serious.

The drive to Texas A&M took about an hour and a half. I called four friends and asked them to pray for him. Then I called Lindsey and left a message: *"Checote's having trouble with his leg. I'm on my way to A&M right now."*

She called back within minutes. "There's not enough blood flow to his leg," she said. "He's developed a bacterial infection."

That was exactly what I'd feared. I asked if she thought it had reached the bone. Early in his recovery, we'd worried about that possibility.

"No," she said quickly. "It's not in the bone – it's all superficial, just in the scar tissue. I've pulled the infection and the bad bacteria out. I watched it float away."

That's exactly how she said it.
I watched it float away.

I asked about the blackened area on his leg. "It's just an old bruise," she said. "Nothing to worry about."

Then with obvious concern, Lindsey said "But why is there so little blood flow all of a sudden?"

I told her I'd noticed the scar tissue had looked paler in recent months, not its usual healthy pink. She tuned in to Checote and said softly, "He feels weaker than he used to. He doesn't think he's the same horse anymore. He doesn't believe he can defend himself."

I then knew exactly why. Six months earlier, while visiting a friend's ranch, Checote had been chased by another horse, and he ran through a fence. He'd escaped with only a small chest hematoma, but he was shaken to his core – he became depressed, withdrawn, eyes dull.

As we talked, I asked, "Does he know where I'm taking him?"

"Yes," Lindsey said. "He's worried. He's afraid they'll cut on him again."

I couldn't blame him. Half the time we'd gone to A&M, he'd ended up in surgery. I reassured her that I didn't expect that to happen this time.

"I've given him what he needs," she said. "He'll be okay for the visit."

And she was right.

When we arrived at the hospital, something extraordinary happened.

For the first time in his life, Checote walked straight into the building without hesitation. No balking at the doorway. No wide-eyed fear of the sterile hallways. He stepped onto the scale with only a brief pause, then followed me into the exam room like he trusted every step.

It was almost eerie.

Then the vet unwrapped his leg.

And I stared.

The swelling – the grotesque balloon of fluid and heat that had terrified me – was already more than halfway gone. The leg was cool. Calm. Normal-looking, for him anyway.

There was no heat.
No redness.
No pus.
No fever.

I touched it myself, hardly believing it.

"If his leg had looked like this," I told the vet, "I wouldn't have brought him in tonight."

She gave me a look of polite disbelief – until she saw the polo wrap with a lot of dried pus still clinging to it.

Her expression changed then. She believed me.

The vet nodded slowly. "The black area is just an old bruise – nothing serious."

The next day, Dr. Rakestraw called after examining Checote and running a full set of tests. "I can't find any sign of infection," he said. "Almost no swelling, no fever. From your description, it sounds like he had a bacterial infection that resolved itself."

Resolved itself.

That was fine by me. Overreaction or not, my horse's leg looked nearly normal again.

Once again, Lindsey had been right.

He asked what had prompted the emergency trip.

I explained every detail – the massive swelling, the feverish heat, the pus, the pain.

“I believe you,” he said kindly. “Horses can surprise us.”

He was kind, as always, but I could tell he thought I’d overreacted.

But I knew the truth.

I had seen the swelling.
I had felt the heat.
I had *smelled* the infection.
And then… I had watched it disappear.

Lindsey had been right.
Again.

The next day, as I walked Checote out of the hospital, my hand resting on his neck, I whispered, “Thank you, Boy, for holding on. And thank you, Lindsey… wherever you are right now.”

Most of all, thank you GOD. Because my horse was still alive, and he was going to be ok… again.

Once again, the unseen had reached out and helped him when he needed it most.

Chapter Five – Life With Checote

The Carrot Thief

It started as one of those slow, golden Texas Sundays – the kind where the heat sits soft on your shoulders and the world feels just a little kinder. After church, after errands, after life had gotten done nudging me around all morning, I stopped at the grocery store and grabbed a big bunch of carrots for the horses.

Not the ordinary bagged kind.
The good kind – the kind with leafy green tops that look like something a cartoon rabbit would dream about.

Checote *loved* those. Coco did too. And I always liked bringing them something bright and crunchy to end the weekend with.

By the time I pulled into the barn, the sun was dipping low enough to cast long shadows across the arena. We had a good ride that afternoon – relaxed, easy, the sort of ride that felt more like breathing than effort. When we finished, I gathered Coco's lead rope in one hand, slung the grocery sack over the other, and started walking them both toward their turnout.

Checote, as usual, followed behind me with his lead rope draped casually across his back, completely unrestrained and utterly trustworthy. He knew the routine. He knew where he was going. And he knew – with that mischievous glint he got sometimes – exactly when I was distracted.

One of the carrot tops stuck up over the edge of the grocery bag, bobbing with every step I took.

Apparently, it was more temptation than Checote could stand.

I didn't see him do it. Not the snaking neck, not the sneaky stretch of his nose, not the delicate, almost surgical way he lifted the carrot from the bag like a pickpocket stealing a watch. But I heard someone behind me laugh and shout:

"Hey! Look at Checote!"

I spun around.

And there he was.

HIDING behind Coco's rump like a guilty toddler, the entire carrot dangling sideways from his mouth – green leaves tickling the corner of his cheek – and the BIGGEST expression of innocence I have ever seen on a horse.

He glanced at me, eyes wide, ears perked, as if to say:

What? Who, me? I didn't take anything.

I burst out laughing so loud the horses flicked their ears in surprise.

Coco, meanwhile, nearly lost her mind. She snorted, stomped, craned her neck toward him, practically vibrating with jealousy.

Because if there was one universal truth in her world, it was this:

If Checote has a treat, Coco also deserves a treat. Immediately.

When I finally got them into their turnout, Coco was still pestering him. So I decided fairness mattered – Checote had cheated, so Coco got the first carrot. She devoured hers so fast the orange crunch barely registered before it was gone.

Then I pulled out another carrot and handed it to Checote.

And that's when the magic happened.

He took the orange end for himself, holding it carefully between his teeth. Then, with a deliberate little twist of his neck, he turned toward Coco…

…and **offered her the leafy tops** like a gentleman presenting flowers.

She leaned over and plucked them right out of his mouth with the daintiest nibble I'd ever seen from her.

I blinked, stunned.

Then I laughed again – harder this time – because it was the sweetest, strangest, most heart-melting thing I had ever witnessed.

A horse feeding another horse.

Not fighting.
Not snatching.
Not stealing.

Feeding.
Sharing.
Loving.

After that, it became their little ritual.
Every carrot I gave him:

Carrot for me.
Leaves for you.

He didn't hesitate.
She didn't hesitate.
And I just stood there, the world's most entertained spectator, wondering how on earth I'd gotten lucky enough to witness such a thing.

In all my years around horses – decades of barns, pastures, trail rides, and training – I had *never* seen one horse feed another except a mare feeding her foal.

But that was Checote.

He broke rules.
He broke expectations.
He broke every idea I ever had of what a horse was supposed to be.

He loved big.
He loved gently.
And sometimes, he loved through carrots.

Even now, all these years later, that memory still makes me laugh out loud. I can see him clearly – that guilty, funny expression as he hid behind Coco with the carrot hanging from his lips. And then the tenderness, the careful tilt of his head as he offered her the greens.

Some horses steal your carrots.

Mine shared them.

The One Who Wanted to Swim

We went riding one afternoon at my friend's 800-acre ranch in Hearne, Texas. My friend, Mary was riding Coco, and as we rode, we started talking about swimming with our horses. I told her how much Checote loves the water – how I'd swam with him a few times before his accident and how much he'd enjoyed every second of it.

Not long after, we came to a large pond and decided to let the horses wade in for a drink. They weren't particularly interested in drinking, but Checote had other ideas. The moment we stepped into the water, he kept wanting to go farther and farther out.

The pond bottom was the thick, sticky kind of mud that tries to suck your boots off, and I couldn't tell how deep the water might get. Worried that it could turn into quicksand or drop off suddenly, I turned him back toward the bank.

But Checote wasn't giving up easily – he was determined to go deeper. When I felt him start to lower his head and shift his weight, I realized what he was thinking. He was about to lie down – *with me on him!*

That was enough for me. "No, sir! We are not swimming today!" I laughed as I guided him out of the water.

Just as we got back to the bank, our friends Brigitta and Linda caught up and rode their horses into the pond.

Within seconds, and in one smooth, ridiculous motion, Linda's horse folded his legs and laid *right down* in the water. Completely. One whole side of his body disappeared under the mud. Linda barely had time to fling herself off, landing in knee-deep water with a shriek that turned into laughter.

It was so absurd, so unexpected, that Mary, Brigitta and I bent over our saddles laughing until our stomachs hurt.

"See?" I said to Checote, wiping tears from my face. "This is why we don't swim every day. You'd have way too much fun."

He flicked an ear, pretending innocence.

Perfect's muddy side after laying down in the pond

The next day, back at Callegari, we rode out to the creek crossing – a winding ribbon of water slicing through the wooded trails. The path led directly between two banks, shallow and safe.

Naturally, that meant nothing to Checote.

The moment his hooves touched water, he veered off the path with laser-focused purpose and plunged himself right into the deeper part of the creek.

"Cote!" I sputtered, laughing. "Stay on the trail!"

He ignored me completely – bliss written all over his face as he splashed deeper, lifting his legs high like a child stomping puddles.

He wasn't drinking.
He wasn't cooling off.
He was *trying to swim again.*

"Oh, you little turkey," I said, laughing helplessly. "You're doing this on purpose."

And he was.

Every part of him said so – the eager prance, the alert ears, the slight wiggle of excitement through his shoulders. If he could've spoken English, he would've yelled, *Let's go for a dip!*

A few weeks later, the phone rang.

It was Lindsey.

There was laughter in her voice before she even spoke.

"Tammy," she said, "Checote keeps reaching out to me."

"Oh Lord," I muttered, because when Checote reached out, it was never about something small. "What does he want?"

"He says to tell you…"
She paused for dramatic effect.

"…he wants to go swimming."

I burst out laughing. "Of course he does! Tell him now it's too cold! He'll have to wait until summer!"

Lindsey laughed too. "He is *very* annoyed that it's winter."

"I bet he is," I said, picturing him pouting like a child denied his favorite toy.

If he could have written me a note and taped it to the barn door, I'm convinced it would've read:

WE SHOULD BE SWIMMING.
LOVE, CHECOTE.

He never stopped wanting water. Not even years later. Whether it was a creek, a pond, or a muddy puddle big enough to splatter in, water lit something inside him – something joyful, playful, almost boyish.

He didn't care if it soaked my jeans or splashed up my shirt.
He didn't care if it was messy.
He didn't care if it made no sense.

He wanted to swim because it made him *alive.*

And honestly, I understood.

With everything we'd survived together – the injury, the surgeries, the long slow climb back – there was something beautiful in seeing him embrace joy with such unrestrained enthusiasm.

Checote didn't just survive life.

He lived it.
He chased it.
He dove straight into it – mud, water, laughter and all.

And every time he pulled me toward water, every time he tried to dip a little deeper or splash a little harder, he reminded me of something simple and true:

Joy isn't something you wait for.
It's something you wade into.

Sometimes ankle-deep.
Sometimes all the way to your shoulders.

And sometimes –
if you're lucky enough to have a horse like Checote –
you swim.

Impact Injury During Farrier Visit

Over the years, my work has taken me on the road quite a bit, and as a result, I haven't always been home when Howard came to shoe or trim my horses. I don't tend to worry about it since Howard is so good, and my horses are used to him.

On one such trip, I returned home to find Checote standing quietly in his stall – but something wasn't right. He was stiff and stoved up, favoring one side. The farrier had been out while I was away, and someone else had held Checote for him that day.

It was clear Checote was in pain. Worried, I called Lindsey to see if she could tune into him. As soon as she answered, I could hear the concern in her voice. After a few moments of quiet, she said, "He lost his balance during his farrier visit and slammed his foot hard into the ground. The shock went all the way up into his shoulder."

"Put your hand on the shoulder," she said. "No – higher. A little to the right. Stop. There."

I pressed my palm into the exact spot she indicated.

Checote flinched – barely, but enough for me to know.
We'd found it.

"That's the place," Lindsey said. "That's where the energy is stuck."

"Now what?"

"Massage it out. Slow circles. He'll tell you when you're doing it right."

So I did.

At first, the muscle felt like knotted rope – tight, unforgiving. But as I worked, heat bloomed under my fingers. Not just warmth – *heat*, rising like something alive. My palms tingled. My wrists buzzed. It felt as if energy was pouring out of me in a steady, pulsing stream.

Checote let out a long, soft sigh.

His head dropped.

His lower lip quivered the way it always did when he was releasing tension.

"That's good," Lindsey said in my ear. "Keep going…"

I don't know how long I worked that shoulder – ten minutes, fifteen, maybe more. All I knew was the softer the muscle became, the easier his breathing grew, and the calmer *I* felt.

Then, almost suddenly, the tightness vanished beneath my hand.

He lifted his head, blinked slowly, and shifted his weight again.

This time, there was no hesitation.

"Try walking him," Lindsey said.

I led him out of his stall.

He walked sound.

He walked freely.

He walked like nothing had ever happened.

Just twenty minutes earlier, he had looked like a horse bracing against pain. Now he was relaxed and fluid again, swinging through his shoulder as if the stiffness had been nothing but a passing thought.

I don't know why after all this time I was stunned. But I still was.

"He's okay," I whispered.

"He will be," Lindsey said. "He just needed help releasing it. And he trusts you enough to let it go."

I rested my forehead against his neck, breathing in the warm, familiar smell of dust and hay and horse.

“Thank you,” I said softly – to Lindsey, yes, but also to the horse who had once again let me into his pain and allowed me to help lift it away.

He turned his head just slightly, brushing his muzzle close to my face.

His way of saying *thank you too.*

And in that quiet stall, with the last light fading outside and the world slowing to a hush, I understood something I hadn’t known before:

Healing wasn’t always surgery.
It wasn’t always medicine.
Sometimes healing lived in the invisible space between two souls
–
in trust, in touch,
in the simple belief that love itself could make things right again.

Chapter Six - The Angels

Lindsey moved away far too soon.

One day she was there – riding beside me, laughing on Saturday mornings, always on the lookout for ways to help – and then life pulled her somewhere else. I missed her more than I expected to. I missed her presence, and the way she seemed to understand my animals in a way that felt like sunlight breaking through leaves. More than anything, I missed my friend.

Without her, the barn felt different. Not empty, just… quieter.

It was a few months later when a new woman arrived with her horse. The barn aisle was warm that afternoon – the kind of heat that makes the dust hang in the air like tiny motes of gold. I had just filled Checote's bucket with water, because he still prefers the bucket to the automatic waterers, and I was carrying it back toward his stall when I saw her.

A petite woman with silver-gray hair cut in a cute bob, a halter draped over one forearm, her expression open and curious as she watched the comings and goings around her. She smiled when our eyes met.

"Hi there," she said. "I'm Bee. I just moved in."

I returned the smile. "I'm Tammy. Welcome to the madhouse." We laughed, because everyone knows every barn is its own kind of madhouse.

She glanced at the bucket in my hand. "Which horses are yours?"

"Those two," I said, nodding toward the stalls across the aisle. "Checote and Coco."

The moment her eyes landed on Checote's stall, something changed. Her face went slack – surprised, almost startled – and for a breath or two she simply stared.

"That's *your* horse?" she asked, pointing toward Checote as if afraid to be wrong.

"Yes," I said slowly. "That's my boy."

She drew in a soft breath, the kind people make when something unexpected and profound sweeps through them.

"I need to tell you something," she said quietly. "I hope you won't think I'm crazy."

At a barn, that's rarely a promising start.
But something in her tone made me set the bucket down.

"I can see angels," she continued, "and there are two angels in that stall. Right there with him. They don't leave him. Ever."

For a moment, neither of us moved. The air between us felt charged, like the hush right before thunder.

Then I smiled – not surprised, not doubtful, just warm.

"I know," I said.

Her eyes widened. "You… know?"

I nodded. "He's never alone. Not anymore."

Bee studied me, as if trying to decide whether I was humoring her or speaking a deeper truth. Whatever she saw in my face made her shoulders relax. She smiled back, gently.

"Well," she said softly, "that's good. I was just so surprised, because it's rare to see an animal with its own angel. And, I've NEVER seen one with TWO angels before."

I carried the bucket into Checote's stall as Bee walked away, her footsteps quiet on the aisle's concrete. Checote lifted his head when I stepped inside, ears flicking toward me, his warm breath brushing my arm as he nudged the water bucket.

I ran my hand along his neck, feeling the familiar strength there. "Of course you have two angels," I whispered. "Of course you do."

A Thread Of Light

A few weeks later, the evening light slanted through the barn doors, casting long golden beams across the hitching post where I was grooming Checote. The smell of feed, hay and shavings mingled with the soft swish of his tail. He dozed lightly as I brushed him, his lower lip loose, one hind hoof resting.

Bee walked by, paused, and simply watched us for a moment.

Then she said something that made the whole world stop.

"You and your horse," she murmured. "The bond between you is so strong… I can see it. There's a thread of light running from your forehead to his. It's… shimmering. Like it's alive."

I didn't speak at first. I just stood with my hand on Checote's shoulder, letting her words settle into the quiet between us.

A thread of light.

A visible connection.

Part of me wanted to laugh because I was so excited about it, but most of me simply believed her. Not because she said it – but because I had always felt it. A pull, a knowing, a constant prcsence between us that needed no explanation.

I turned toward Checote. He lifted his head and placed his muzzle close to my face where we breathed the same air. He still often did that in quiet moments together. He still liked to share my air.

"Yeah," I whispered. "I feel it too."

Bee smiled softly.
Some people hear angels.
Some people see them.
Some people just know when they're in the presence of something sacred.

And some horses – like mine – carry a light so strong that the rest of us can only marvel at it.

In that moment, with the fading sunlight, I realized something:

What Bee saw
…was what my heart had always known.

Checote wasn't just my horse.
He was a blessing.
And love – real love – leaves a light in the world, whether we see it or not.

Tammy & Checote

A New Angel

Saturday lunches were our ritual.

After every group ride – dusty boots, sweaty shirts and filthy jeans – we'd pile into our trucks or cars and head to our favorite restaurant since it could tolerate half-feral horse people smelling of sweat, leather, and hay. Usually, we'd fill a long table with too many chairs and too much laughter.

But on this particular Saturday, it was only Bee and me. Everyone else had scattered – family plans, early errands, unexpected chores. So the two of us ended up at a small table tucked into the corner of our favorite local restaurant, the kind with warm chips, icy tea, and the low hum of conversation drifting around us like background music.

We ordered our food, chatted about little nothings, and settled into the comfortable quiet that happens when you don't need to fill every space with words.

Halfway through the meal, as I reached for my iced tea, Bee went still.

She looked up suddenly, eyes unfocused – like she was hearing something far away.

Then, in a soft voice, she said,
"Checote just got another angel."

My hand hovered in midair. "Another one? Do you mean… replacing the other two?" I asked.

She shook her head slowly. "No. In addition to them. The first two never leave him – they're always with him. But this new angel…"

she paused, listening inwardly again, "…this one has a different purpose."

My breath caught. "What purpose?"

"To help him," she said. "But also to help someone else – through him."
She met my eyes, her expression unusually solemn. "This angel is meant to guide him. It's something he must do. Checote is going to have to help someone."

Her words settled over the table like a weight.

I tried to swallow it down, nodding slowly, pretending it made sense. But unease prickled at the base of my neck.

"Help someone?," I echoed. "Who? Why?"

Bee shook her head. "I can't see that part. Only that it will matter. And it's close."

I fell quiet. The restaurant noise faded until all I could hear was the clink of dishes and the distant hum of a ceiling fan.

At the time, I thought I understood.
I thought the angel was for me.

I worried constantly about my father – his heart problems, his fragile health. And something deep in my gut, something I didn't want to name, whispered that my marriage wasn't as whole as I pretended it was. I was afraid the angel was meant to brace me for pain I didn't see coming yet, but could feel like a storm on the horizon.

I didn't tell Bee that part. That part was very private.
But, I didn't have to. The way she looked at me told me she already knew more than I was saying.

We finished our meal quietly, both of us soft-spoken, as if neither wanted to disturb whatever unseen thing had entered our conversation.

When we left the restaurant, the sun outside was blinding. Heat radiated off the pavement, shimmering like a mirage. I blinked against it and took a deep breath, trying to shake the strange heaviness clinging to me.

But the feeling stayed.

Something was coming.
Something big.
Something meant for Checote – and for me.

I didn't know it then, but in ten days, his new angel would reveal exactly why it had arrived.

And everything in my world was about to change again.

Chapter Seven - Finding Jean

Riding with the bareback pad

About ten days after Bee told me Checote had received a new angel, I arrived at the barn after work. It was a very warm evening, and I was in shorts and tennis shoes – I had no intention of riding. As I was pulling Checote out of his stall, I saw two horses galloping into the barnyard, still saddled but riderless. My heart stopped. They belonged to my friends, Jean and Brigitta.

I ran to catch them and handed their reins to someone nearby, then I threw a bridle and bareback pad on Checote. Within moments, we were on the trail.

There was no saddle. No boots. No time to waste.
Just me, my horse, and a sudden, overwhelming certainty:

Jean is hurt. And we have to find her.

The trail system beside our barn was a labyrinth of winding paths and endless forks. And since I wasn't there when they hit the trail, there was no way to know which way Jean and Brigitta had gone.

So I did the only thing I could – I laid the reins down on Checote's neck and said, "***Find Jean. Jean is hurt. Find Jean***."

The Search Begins

He immediately turned right at the trailhead, then took the first left toward the creek. We went down the steep embankment to the water, then he crossed the creek, turned left again, then took a right at the next fork – a path we *never* used. That trail led straight into a gravel quarry filled with heavy machinery, clanging metal, and roaring engines. It's a place you *don't* ride a horse. But I trusted him.

He knew.

The evening sun dipped low, throwing long shadows across the trail as he trotted toward the massive clearing of stone and machinery ahead. Then he headed left and straight for the gravel pit.

Guided by Something Unseen

We reached the brim of the gravel pit – a high ridge overlooking a sprawling industrial bowl scarred by excavators, conveyor belts, and mountains of crushed rock.

The moment his hooves hit the rim, Checote broke into a dead run.

Wind tore at my hair and clothes. The world blurred. My fingers dug into his thick mane. We had not run this fast since before his accident.

And for a heartbeat – just one – I saw it:

A flicker of light ahead of us.
Soft.
Golden.
Moving with purpose.

An angel leading the way. I knew then this was his mission.

I didn't doubt it for a second.

The Stop

Halfway around the pit, Checote slid to a stop. I looked around but saw nothing. Then I pulled out my phone and called Brigitta. She answered instantly.
"I'm right below you," she said.

I looked down into the pit and saw them. Jean was lying on the ground, badly injured – her shoulder shattered.

As it turns out, the path that Checote took through the gravel quarry, was the quickest and most direct route to reach them.

We rode down the steep wall of the pit to see how we could help.

Brigitta asked me to ride out and flag down the rescue vehicles. I could already hear faint sirens in the distance. My heart clenched. There was no time to waste.

Guiding the Rescue Trucks

Checote exploded into motion, charging up the gravel pit wall and circling the pit at a full run back toward the gravel quarry.

We raced around the pit's rim, the ground vibrating beneath us. At the far end of the quarry, we reached the maze of machinery.

A towering conveyor belt roared overhead, dumping mountains of gravel into a metal bin the size of a house. The sound was deafening – metal on metal, gravel pounding like thunder.

Checote trotted under it as calmly as if we were on a Sunday trail ride.

Next came the two ponds – long, deep pits of water used for the quarry's operations. Between them lay a huge hose, thick as a fire line, pumping water from one pond to the other. It vibrated violently on the ground, thrumming like a living thing.

Checote stepped over it without hesitation.

Nothing frightened him.
Nothing slowed him.
He was a horse on a mission.

We reached the road. I waved down the first rescue truck, breathless, pointing them toward the quarry. The driver followed us, but the terrain was too rough for him to keep up. I kept slowing Checote so they wouldn't lose us.

After delivering the first truck, they asked us to fetch the ambulance and the second rescue team.

We made two more runs.

Each time, Checote pushed harder, faster – and each time I felt that same strange certainty: **We aren't doing this alone.**

Through it all, Checote never faltered. Not once. He was on a mission, and nothing – not pain, noise, heat, or exhaustion – would stop him.

The Aftermath

Once we guided the final rescue truck, we were told to leave the scene. Checote was dripping white lather. He hadn't run that far, that fast, or that hard since before his accident. We walked slowly toward the creek to cool him down.

As we crossed the water, I spotted a large turtle that had flipped upside down, and it was kicking helplessly. Another soul in need of rescue. I slipped off Checote, used the toe of my shoe to gently turn the turtle upright, and smiled as it crawled away.

When I tried to remount, I realized I couldn't – not bareback, not from the ground without stirrups on a saddle. I am too short. I led Checote to a sand pile to use as a mounting block. The sand gave way beneath me, and I fell flat underneath him. He looked down between his legs and I heard him say, *What on earth are you doing down there?*

Eventually, I found a rock sturdy enough to climb back on. By the time we reached the barn, Checote was still covered in foam. I led him in slow circles to help him cool off before rinsing him down.

One of the other boarders ran up, wide-eyed. "What happened?" he asked.

I told him the story – how Checote had found Jean, led the rescuers, and never wavered once.

He just shook his head and said, "Checote's just like Lassie!"

And he was right. That night, my brave little horse and his new angel fulfilled their purpose.

Later that evening, as I brushed Checote's coat, I realized what Bee's words had meant. The new angel hadn't come to protect *me* – it had come to guide *him* when the moment called for courage beyond instinct.

Checote had followed something greater than sight or sound that day. He had followed faith. Together, we'd been part of something extraordinary – proof that love, trust, and a little divine guidance can move through even the smallest of creatures to do the greatest of things.

I looked into his eyes and whispered, “You did it, Cote. You found her.”

He simply lowered his head, shared my air, and said, *I know.*

Jean on her horse, Chiquita

Chapter Eight - The Breaking Point

After Checote found Jean, I thought maybe his mission was over. I told Bee about what had happened, how he had followed some unseen path through the woods, how he'd run like something was guiding him.

Bee listened quietly, her eyes distant, as if she could see beyond what I was describing.
"Was that it?" I asked her. "Was that the mission you were talking about?"

She smiled faintly, but there was sadness in her expression.
"That was one of them," she said softly. "But the angel isn't gone yet."

A chill ran through me. "Then who does he have to help now?"

Her gaze met mine. "You," she said.

I wanted to ask what she meant, but her tone stopped me. Some things, I've learned, you're not meant to understand until you have to.

A few months later, my world cracked open. I found out my husband had been cheating on me. The discovery was devastating for me – and created a hollow ache that spread through my chest like smoke. The divorce that followed was slow and cruel, the kind of pain that bleeds and burns.

The Refuge

Through it all, I kept going to the barn. It was the only place that still felt steady. Checote would lift his head the moment he heard my truck door close, his ears pricking forward, his soft whinny always greeting me.

I'd press my face against his neck, the smell of hay and dust and horse sweat grounding me in a way nothing else could. He didn't move, didn't flinch – just breathed, long and slow, as if reminding me to do the same, and he shared my air. And I heard him. *I'm still here. You're not alone.*

Protecting Him From My Pain

Over the next weeks, as the divorce unfolded piece by piece, I leaned on Checote more than ever – but always with quiet caution. He had already endured so much in his life, and I refused to let my darkness spill over onto him. I didn't want my grief to weigh on him, or confuse him, or dull the golden light he carried.

So I learned to hold myself together around him, to breathe deeply before walking down the barn aisle, to offer him steady hands even when my heart was trembling.

But he knew.
He always knew.

He would lift his head over the stall door the moment he heard my footsteps, ears pricked forward, eyes soft and knowing. Every time I tried to smile for him, he would nicker quietly, as if acknowledging the lie.

When I leaned my forehead against his, he would close his eyes and breathe slowly – deep breaths that matched the ones he taught me to take.

And on the days when the sadness threatened to swallow me whole, I climbed onto his back and let him carry me into the wind.

Riding Out the Heartbreak

Checote

On the trail, with my hands buried in his thick mane and the rhythm of his hooves beneath me, the world softened. The wind tugged at my hair, and the trees opened their quiet arms to us. When he ran – really ran – it felt like he was trying to lift me out of myself, to pull my grief into the air where it could dissolve.

Every gallop was a release.
Every exhale was freedom.
Every moment with him reminded me that life could still hold beauty, even when everything else seemed broken.

I don't know how I would've survived that time without him. Honestly, I don't think I could have.

And in those long, painful months, I began to understand exactly what Bee meant when she said that angel wasn't sent only to guide him.

It was sent to guide him **to me.**

When I climbed on his back, everything fell away. The moment he broke into a trot, the wind tore through my hair and my grief, and for those few precious minutes, I wasn't the woman whose marriage had fallen apart. I was just *me* again – alive, weightless, flying.

Looking back, I realize that Checote's greatest gift to me wasn't just his strength or his courage – it was his presence. He never tried to fix my pain; he simply stood beside me and carried me through it. In his quiet way, he reminded me that love doesn't always come to change what hurts – sometimes it simply stays, steady and sure, until the hurt begins to fade.

Love has a way of finding you when you think it's gone. Sometimes it doesn't come in words or promises – sometimes it comes in the steady breath of a horse beneath you, in the trust of a friend who carries you through every storm without question. Checote didn't heal me by changing what had happened. He healed me by staying, by letting me lean on him until I remembered how to stand again.

The Hornets' Nest

The trail was quiet the day Checote and I rode into the hornets' nest – the kind of late afternoon where the sun settles low and the air hangs still. We were riding a narrow path cut along a steep embankment, the kind where you don't look down unless you want your stomach to drop. On one side, the ground rose sharply; on the other, it fell away into a long slope toward the water below.

It was the sort of trail you only ride on a horse you trust with your life.

For me, that was always Checote.

We were halfway along a bend in the path, when the world suddenly erupted into a furious buzzing. A cloud of hornets burst from a hidden nest burrowed into the embankment on one side of us – and we rode straight through them.

They struck instantly.

I felt them slam into Checote's neck, his shoulders, even his head. They stung him in a frenzy, one after another. I could hear the angry hum all around us, see the blur of wings as they attacked.

But not a single one touched me.

Checote flinched as the first stinger hit, then another, and another. He shook his head violently, trying to dislodge them, but he never – not even for a heartbeat – broke stride.

He didn't bolt.
He didn't panic.
He didn't take a single reckless step.

The trail was too dangerous for mistakes. One misstep on that narrow ledge and we could have gone tumbling down the embankment into the water far below.

Even while hornets swarmed his face and neck, he stayed steady beneath me – choosing every careful hoof placement with deliberate precision, absorbing the pain without risking my safety.

I could feel his body trembling from the stings, muscles tightening and releasing under the saddle. But still he walked forward, ears pinned, shaking his head when he had to, but never letting fear drive his feet.

It wasn't until we cleared the nest and the last of the hornets peeled away that he released a long, shuddering breath.

Only then did he allow himself to stop.

I slid off immediately and moved around to check him. Angry red welts were already rising across his neck and along the crest of his mane, some swelling fast, others already hot to the touch. He blew out softly, lowering his head so I could see the stings near his jaw.

And then – despite all the pain he was clearly in – he nudged me gently, checking *me*.

I wrapped my arms around his neck, holding him as tightly as I dared. He had taken every sting, every bit of pain, and never let a single one touch me.

He protected me when instinct alone could have led him to run blind through danger.
He kept me safe on a trail where panic could have killed us both.
He chose courage over instinct – and chose *me* over his own pain.

That was the kind of horse he was.

My guardian.
My protector.
My brave, steady-hearted partner.

And as I stood there with my face pressed into his mane, I whispered, "Thank you, Cote. You saved me."

He lowered his head again, and said, *I always will.*

Chapter Nine - The Next Stage of Life

Home at my new ranch

After the divorce, I packed what little of my life still felt like mine and moved to the country.
Just a small patch of land - barely enough to impress anyone, but more than enough to heal me. It was quiet. Honest. Real. The kind of place where the nights smelled of trees, freshly cut fields and damp earth; and the mornings felt like fresh beginnings instead of leftovers from the day before.

Best of all, I brought my horses home.

For the first time in my life, I was Checote and Coco's full-time caretaker - no boarders, no barns, no facility staff between us. Just me, my horses, and the wide Texas sky. I hadn't known how badly my soul needed that kind of peace until I felt it for the first time. Sitting out on my back deck at dusk, watching Checote and Coco graze on land that I first rented and eventually owned… it was a kind of serenity I didn't even recognize at first. It wasn't happiness or excitement or relief.

It was steading, it was grounding, it was “Home”.

Sometimes I’d wrap my hands around a warm cup of tea at sunrise or sunset and just listen to the quiet: the soft rip of grass between the horses’ teeth, the occasional contented snort, the flap of a bird’s wings as it crossed the fence line. Those were the moments that made me feel whole again – as if life had gently placed me back where I belonged.

I had thought I would bring Leah home with me as well. I wanted her with me in this next chapter of my life. But she passed away just a week after I moved in. Losing her hit me harder than I expected. Leah was the horse who brought horses back into my life all those years ago. She single-hoofedly pulled me out of a terrible depression after my divorce from another cheating husband. I used to joke, “I got a divorce and got a horse – it was a good trade.” But the truth is, Leah saved me. She taught me so much. Not as much as Checote would later teach me, but she was the one who set me on the path to the life I was meant to live.

After being at the ranch for about a year, something in me shifted. I found myself stepping into rescue work. At first, I adopted a couple of horses from a wonderful organization, the Bluebonnet Equine Humane Society. Then I found myself “bailing” horses out of kill pens – saving them from the worst fate a horse can face. I adopted several, and somehow, I was blessed with incredible luck. Every horse I brought home turned out to be something special. Each one found their place in my life, and I found a piece of myself in each of them. Over the years, I have pulled 14 horses directly from the kill pens. Some I have rehomed, where they had a better situation than I could even offer. Most of them became mine for the rest of their natural life.

Hearing Without Ears

By then, the extraordinary experiences I'd had with Sonya Fitzpatrick, and then with Lindsey, had opened a door inside me I hadn't even known was locked. They helped me understand that communication didn't always have to be spoken. That sometimes, if you were willing to be still, to truly listen, you could hear your animals in a way that defied logic but felt completely natural.

I realized that the random, sudden thoughts that popped into my mind – the ones that felt too direct, too urgent, too "not me" – often weren't mine at all.

Learning that was one thing.
Learning to sort my own thoughts from theirs… well, that was another matter entirely.

Some days it still feels like trying to catch smoke with my hands. Other days, the messages come through so clearly that there is absolutely no mistaking them.

That lesson was driven home one year on the Salt Grass Trail Ride.

The Call I Couldn't Ignore

Riding Coco on the Salt Grass Trail Ride

After a long day in the saddle, I was sitting at the cookshack with friends, eating dinner, swapping stories, and letting the companionship warm my bones. I had ridden Coco that year, and she was tied to my trailer behind us with her hay bag, bucket of water, and her evening grain.

It was a comfortable night – cool air, the murmur of conversation, the comforting clatter of pots in the cookshack.

And then, out of nowhere, a wave of distress slammed into me.

It wasn't mine.
I knew that immediately.

I heard Coco.

Not with my ears – with something deeper, sharper, the same sense that had been slowly awakening inside me ever since Lindsey came into my life.

I bolted up from my chair so fast the table shook.

I didn't think. I just ran.

By the time I reached her, she was already pawing and stretching, her flanks tightening, her nostrils flaring – every sign of colic written across her body like a warning.

I didn't hesitate. I grabbed my banamine, administered it, and started walking her in slow circles, keeping her legs moving and her mind calm. My hands shook, not with fear, but with urgency – that primal instinct that comes from knowing an animal is relying on you.

Even as I walked her, I pulled out my phone and called Lindsey.

She answered immediately.

"Coco's colicking," I said breathlessly. "It came on fast."

I didn't have to explain. Lindsey grew quiet, tuning in from hundreds of miles away.
"She's dehydrated," she said at last. "She doesn't like the water they're providing. It tastes different. Tell her she needs to drink it anyway."

I looked at Coco – sweating lightly now, but still walking. "You hear that, girl? You need to drink. Please drink."

I didn't know how Lindsey did what she did. I still don't. But within minutes, Coco dipped her muzzle into the water bucket and began to drink.

It was a lesson I've never forgotten:
Always bring water from home when you travel with horses.

Coco was one of Checote's Angel's. This was proof that even Angels need an angel of their own sometimes.

Becoming What I Already Was

Lindsey had been telling me for years that I was not only a natural teacher – something I'd always known about myself – but also a natural healer.

I didn't believe her.

I thought she meant I was good at comforting people, listening when they were hurting. Friends often told me I made them feel better. I figured that was all Lindsey meant.

She insisted it was more.

At the time, I couldn't see it.
Not until Coco proved it to me.

The Second Colic

Years later, I "heard" Coco again.

The same sudden thought, the same unmistakable sense of distress – sharp and urgent in the center of my mind.

I threw open the back door and ran into the yard. There she was, standing by the fence line near the back gate, waiting for me, shifting uneasily, her belly tight, her breathing shallow.

Another colic.

This time, as I had the banamine ready to administer – something in me whispered, *Wait.*

Instead, I stepped in close and wrapped my arms around her belly, resting my cheek against her warm side. I closed my eyes and listened. Not to her heartbeat or her breath – but to the feeling. The impression that filled my thoughts.

A gas colic.
That's what kept repeating in my mind.

So I prayed.
Not a formal prayer – just intention, focus, and a deep, almost desperate love for this mare who had traveled so many miles with me.

I imagined the gas moving through her body.
Imagined it leaving.
Imagined her relief.

And then it happened.

She passed gas – loudly, forcefully – and immediately exhaled, her whole body softening beneath my hands.

Her pain was gone.

Coincidence?
Maybe.

But standing in the quiet of my backyard that night, with Coco leaning her head against my shoulder in gratitude, I felt something click inside me. Something shift, open, awaken.

Maybe Lindsey had seen something in me long before I ever saw it in myself.

Maybe we are all healers in ways we haven't yet learned to believe.

Swimming at Lake Conroe With The Kids

Swimming with Cheyenne & Kathryn

2014 – There are some days you don't realize will become lifelong memories until you're already knee-deep – literally – in the middle of them. The day I took two teenage girls, Cheyenne and Kathryn, to Lake Conroe to swim the horses was one of those rare, perfect days that stays with you forever.

Both girls were daughters of friends, each of them horse crazy in their own way. One had recently adopted a wild mustang; and the both of them were brand-new to the idea of swimming with horses. I put Cheyenne on Coco, of course. If you wanted a horse who would take flawless care of a beginner in the water, Coco was the only answer. She could read fear, confidence, excitement - whatever her rider felt - and match it exactly.

We rode out into the lake until the water rose high on the horses' sides. Before long we were deep enough that the horses began to float, stepping lightly, then lifting into full swimming strokes. The girls squealed with excitement as we splashed, played, and drifted through the cool water. Their laughter echoed across the lake, mixing with the sound of horses blowing water through their nostrils like children in a bathtub.

Coco was in her element. That mare adored the water. She plunged her entire head under the surface again and again, popping up like a seal, water streaming from her forelock. You had to hang on tight if you wanted to stay with her – when Coco played, she played with her whole heart.

The mustang had fun too, though she watched Coco like she thought the older mare had completely lost her mind. Checote, meanwhile, moved with that calm, steady presence he always carried around the water – alert, gentle, and careful of his people.

I'd brought along a waterproof camera to capture the joy and chaos of the day. But Lake Conroe had other plans for me. While laughing at Coco's underwater antics, I dropped the camera.

We were in deep water – chest-deep on Checote and nearly chin-deep on me. Lake Conroe is not known for its clarity. The bottom is silty and dark, and you can't see more than a few inches down. If anything falls into that water, it might as well have dropped into a black hole.

But I was determined. I wasn't about to lose the pictures of this day.

I asked Checote to *stand still* for me. Then I took a breath and dove. And dove again. And again. I felt blindly across the bottom, sweeping my hands through the murk, knowing full well the tiny current could have carried the camera far away.

Each time I surfaced, Checote was standing exactly where I'd left him – statue-still, ears turned toward me, waiting patiently.

I continued diving and searching. I was swimming under his belly and between his legs. Finally, on one dive, my fingers brushed the edge of something hard. I grabbed it and surfaced triumphantly, sputtering lake water, holding the camera high like a prize.

When I saw where it had been, I could have cried.
It was sitting right next to Checote's front foot.
One shift, one step, one casual movement, and the camera would have been crushed into the silt.

But my boy… he had stayed perfectly still.
He had heard me.
He had understood.
He had honored what I asked of him – just like he always did.

Even with kids laughing, horses splashing, and me diving around his legs like a half-drowned otter, Checote never moved a muscle.

The mustang was a story all her own. Born wild in a roaming herd, gathered up by the BLM, and later sold at auction, she had every reason in the world to distrust humans. But that day on Lake Conroe, she showed nothing but heart. She stood quietly in the water, perfectly balanced and patient, while her young rider – wearing water shoes, soaking wet, and fearless – climbed up onto her back.

Again and again, she let her stand, laugh, and dive off her like she was her very own living diving board. Each time she splashed into the water, she waited for her to resurface, ears forward, as if checking to make sure she was safe. Watching that mustang – wild-born, auction-sold, now trusted beyond measure – was nothing short of beautiful.

Coco was also a living breathing diving board for Cheyenne. All three horses were incredible that day, each of them proving in their own way just how extraordinary horses can be when they choose connection. That moment – more than all the splashing and laughter and fun – was the part that stayed with me. My horses always brought joy into my life, but they also brought trust. Partnership. Understanding. The kind that runs deeper than words.

The girls still talk about that day, and honestly, so do I. It was one of those rare afternoons when everything went exactly right – sun, water, horses, kids, and memories that will last a lifetime.

And somewhere in my photo album is a picture from that very day… taken by the little waterproof camera that survived only because my little Pinto loved me enough to stand perfectly still in the deep waters of Lake Conroe.

Bentley and Bristol

Checote greeting Bentley & Bristol

In August of 2014, I came up with the *brilliant* idea that I needed a pet mini pig. But of course, for reasons I still can't fully explain, I decided that one pig wouldn't do – I needed two so they wouldn't be lonely. So, I adopted two eight-week-old piglets, a brother and sister from the same litter. I named them Bentley and Bristol.

They were quickly litterbox trained, and once they were big enough to use the dog door, they became fully house trained and never once soiled my house. Bentley was the brave one. Bristol was… not. But together they were adorable, smart, and absolute little characters.

Checote adored them. He would often wander into the backyard just to spend time with the pigs. Some of my other horses would chase them if they got too close, but never Checote. He treated every creature with respect and gentleness. Because of that, I always had to be mindful of which horses I allowed into the backyard when Bentley and Bristol were out exploring.

I have a large back deck with steps leading down into the fenced yard. The very first time Bentley – the bold adventurer – decided to leave the deck on his own, it sent poor Bristol into a panic. She came barreling into the house, squealing at the top of her lungs, and found me in the kitchen, cooking at the stove. In all that frantic noise, I somehow understood exactly what she was saying: she couldn't *see* Bentley anymore. He had wandered underneath the deck, out of her line of sight.

I told Bristol I'd be right there, but I needed to pull the food off the burner first. She grunted her acceptance – which cracked me up – and darted back outside. When I finished at the stove and went out, sure enough, Bentley was under the deck. I called him out and asked him to get back up on the deck so he wouldn't scare his sister. And just like that, he did.

A couple of months later, I was upstairs working in my office when Bentley came flying through the dog door. He ran straight to the bottom of the staircase and let out urgent, panicked squeals – and once again, I instantly knew what he meant. Bristol was in trouble. And, I *knew* that her head was stuck in the fence. I raced downstairs and out the back door, and there she was, her head stuck in the fence. And no, this had not happened before. I had to grab wire cutters to free her. We replaced the fencing with chain-link after that so it could never happen again.

What always amazed me was how easily I understood those piglets when they were so young. You'd think, after everything with Checote and my other animals, I wouldn't be surprised by that anymore. But I was. And yet, it's always been the same for me: if one of my animals needs something, somehow, I just *know* what they're trying to tell me.

Chapter Ten – Saying Goodbye

My Dad

April 17, 2013 was the day my father passed away. His heart finally gave out. Losing him was a tremendous heartbreak, and once again, I turned to Checote for comfort.

Before his passing, my dad loved coming to visit me. We would sit together on the back deck for hours, surrounded by the dogs, watching the horses graze in the pasture. Sometimes we'd climb into my mule and ride around the property. The horses would flock to us the moment they saw the mule - nudging in, begging for pets and scratches. My dad just loved it. Those quiet moments with him, the sun setting over the pasture and the horses gathering around, became some of my most treasured memories. I didn't realize then how much I would cling to them later.

My dad always told me that Checote was my prettiest horse. And Cote always wholeheartedly agreed with him.

My parents had divorced many years earlier, and for a long time my dad had lived with a woman who came with two daughters of her own. Over the years, I believed I had grown close to my dad's partner and her daughters - and later to their children, after they married and started families of their own. But when my dad died, things shifted in a way I never saw coming.

There was no estate, no money, no property to fight over. Yet it was as if they felt the few family possessions my dad left behind somehow belonged to them rather than to his own children – my brother, me, and his one and only grandchild. I was blindsided by how quickly they shut me out. They refused to let me have even the smallest family heirlooms, items my dad had told me many times he *wanted* my brother and me to have. None of it was worth anything financially. It was simply sentimental – pieces of my childhood.

My dad had even bronzed the little shoes I learned to walk in. I wasn't even allowed to have those. It felt like a slap in the face on top of losing my hero. And because they cut me out entirely, I also lost the people who had become important to my dad – people I had truly believed were my extended family.

Once again, Checote was right there, steady as ever. In his quiet way, he reminded me of the things that truly matter. Love and Loyalty. I have often found that you get stronger loyalty from an animal than you do people.

In Loving Memory: John D Holsey (Dad)

Saying Goodbye to Coco

2016 – There are moments in a horsewoman's life that leave marks deeper than any scar – moments you feel in your chest every time you think of them. Losing Coco was one of those moments for me. And even now, when I try to explain what she meant to me, words feel small. How do you say goodbye to one of the best riding partners on the planet? How do you say goodbye to one of Checote's Angels? She was his best friend. How do you thank a horse who shaped more lives than most people ever will?

Coco came into my world fourteen years earlier, through my dear friend George Slater. George had raised her from a baby and earned his John Lyons training certification with Coco by his side. That explained everything, because in all my years around horses, I've never met one better trained, more responsive, or more willing than Coco. She was the kind of horse you only get once in a lifetime – if you're lucky.

Her résumé was one for the books. In her younger years, long before I knew her, she was a professional barrel horse, running tight, perfect patterns with the kind of fire that wins buckles. Then she became a professional team roping horse. Then a broodmare who produced a champion roping horse – one who went on to win hundreds of thousands for his ultimate owner. After that she became the ultimate trail horse. Then she was a lesson horse. Then Mary's horse.

I wasn't her official owner back then, but I was her caretaker. I made sure she had what she needed, that she stayed healthy, happy, and understood. In return, she carried Mary safely through every ride. Later, she became Rachael's horse when Sister had to retire. And again - Coco took excellent care of her rider, teaching Rachael how to barrel race and building her confidence, one smooth lap at a time.

That was Coco's magic. She matched herself to whoever sat on her back.
If they were nervous - she was gentle.
If they were learning - she was patient.
If they were experienced - she lit up like the sun.

She gave people their courage back. She made broken riders whole again.

I'll never forget the woman I taught to ride on Coco who was terrified to trot. No matter what I did, Coco wouldn't go faster than a walk. She knew. She felt that fear and refused to let that woman fall apart. Only after the woman relaxed and found her seat did Coco offer the softest, most forgiving trot you could imagine. That was who she was. She protected hearts as much as bodies.

And yet – put an experienced rider on her, and she was a rocket. Smooth at every gait, fast as a flash, and always in control. I used to tell people that running Coco felt like floating. The first time I really opened her up, I thought we were already at full speed until she shifted into another gear I didn't even know existed. The wind was tearing tears from my eyes beneath my sunglasses, and that mare kept reaching, stretching, flying. That day, Coco showed me what wings must feel like.

People said, "Point Coco at a tree and she'll try to climb it for you." They weren't wrong - she would try anything you asked of her, no hesitation.

She carried flags like it was nothing.
She rode bareback like it was her calling.
She loved swimming more than most people love a warm bath on a cold day - especially dunking her head under water like a little kid playing in a bathtub.

And she was always, always willing. Always brave.

When Checote had his devastating accident eleven years ago, Coco became part nurse, part guardian angel. She was careful around him, watching that injured leg closely. And when something was wrong - she let me know. Coco didn't just understand people; she understood other horses too. She understood responsibility.

During the year it took Checote to heal, Coco became my main mount. And she was pure joy. She carried me safely on the Salt Grass Trail Ride when Checote couldn't. She even let me know – loudly – when she started to colic one night on the trail. Coco always told the truth, and I always listened.

We had an understanding, she and I. A deep one.

She hated being tied to a trailer for long stretches, and she used to untie herself and go graze. I explained to her that she couldn't do that on the Salt Grass ride. And after that conversation, she never did it again.
So I made sure to hand graze her each night so she didn't feel trapped.

Respect for respect.
That was our deal.

Coco had a remarkable understanding of the English language. After meeting a new friend, I was explaining her unique ability to comprehend spoken words. To demonstrate, I put Coco in one corner of a large covered arena and asked her to stay. Then I walked all the way to the opposite corner. In the flattest, most casual voice I could manage, I said, *"Coco, would you mind coming over here, please?"*

She immediately turned and walked straight to me.

My friend was impressed, but unconvinced. They insisted it wasn't the *words* she understood, but the *intention behind them.* To make their point, they took Coco to another corner of the arena, walked to the opposite side, and in perfect German said, *"Kommen Sie her, bitte."*

Coco turned and walked straight to them.

My friend looked at me triumphantly and said, *"See? She responds to intention."*

I just smiled and said,
"Oh my gosh! I didn't know Coco spoke German too!"

As she aged, Coco stepped back from her role as the herd's matriarch. She retired from riding and chose Cowboy as her constant companion. Checote stepped into her role as "herd manager". But, he constantly checked on her and looked out for her. Returning the favor after years of her performing as his angel. Those two were a matched set – steady, quiet, deeply connected. He misses her still. Maybe as much as I do.

It was heartbreaking to watch the strong, tank-built mare I loved begin to fade from her own body. Her spirit stayed bright, sharp, aware – but her body simply couldn't keep up anymore. There is a grief in that kind of watching that settles deep in the chest.

But Coco held on gracefully. She held on like the queen she was.

And then, finally… we let go. She let me know it was time.

On the day she passed, I knew – absolutely knew – that her spirit slipped free from that tired, broken-down body and ran straight into the wide, open spaces she always loved. I imagine her swimming in cool, clear waters, tossing her head, splashing, finally weightless. Running beside the wind again. Sound, strong, and whole.

I have no doubt that she joined Checote's other angels to watch over him as they do.
But still…

I miss you, Coco.
Thank you for every mile.
Every ride.
Every lesson.
Every ounce of trust.
You were one of the great ones.

And I will carry you with me for the rest of my life.

Tammy with Checote & Coco

Chapter Eleven - Checote's Retirement

It was 2018. I had been dreaming of it for months – a once-in-a-lifetime horseback adventure with friends.
South Dakota.
Rolling mountains.
Miles of breathtaking trails.
And the ride straight up to Mount Rushmore itself.

It was the kind of trip horse people fantasize about: the long drive, the campfires at night, the smell of leather and pine, the thrill of riding through country that feels bigger than the sky itself. I could hardly contain my excitement. The moment the plans were confirmed, I began telling Checote about it – every last detail, every trail we'd explore, every wide-open view he would love.

I painted pictures in my mind as clearly as if we were already there: the cool northern wind ruffling his mane, the emerald forests, the granite peaks rising above us. I told him how proud I'd be to ride up that mountain with him, my miracle horse, my partner of two decades.

But even as I spoke, I felt a quiet shift inside him – a stillness, a weight, a truth that vibrated through that invisible bond between us.

I can't, he said.

Not in words, but in the deep knowing I'd learned to recognize after all our years together.

His tired, damaged leg – the leg he'd fought to reclaim for nearly thirteen years – simply couldn't handle a trip like that anymore. The trails would be too hard. The climbs too steep. The long days too demanding. His body, though brave beyond measure, had reached its limit.

The realization settled into my chest like a stone.

I didn't want to believe it, but I did.
I heard him loud and clear.

And my heart broke.

After many sleepless nights of thoughts and turmoil, I made the decision I had been avoiding.

I would take Gemini instead.

He was younger, stronger, untouched by catastrophic injury. He had the athleticism and spirit for a trip like South Dakota. It made sense. It was the only option. So I began riding Gemini several times a week, preparing both of us for the journey ahead.

Still, every time I saddled him, a small ache curled behind my ribs – the ache of a chapter closing.

One evening, as the sun dipped low and painted the barnyard in shades of gold, I went out to feed the horses their dinner. Checote and Gemini happened to be in pens right next to each other, their feed buckets clanging softly as they ate.

I walked up to Checote's pen and rested my hands on the top rail.

"Checote," I whispered, "I heard you. I understand. You can't make this trip. It's okay. You've carried me through more than any horse should ever have been asked to. I'm going to take Gemini instead."

He lifted his head slowly from the bucket and turned to look at me. Those beautiful light brown eyes – eyes that had seen storms, miracles, and years of our lives together – held mine for a long, quiet moment.

Then he did something I will never forget.

Checote stepped away from me and walked toward the shared panel between his pen and Gemini's. He lifted his head and reached across the metal rail, stretching toward Gemini.

Gemini raised his head too, meeting Checote halfway until their noses touched.

And in that breathless moment, I heard it as clearly as if they had spoken aloud:

"You better take good care of my girl," Checote told him.

There was no mistaking it – protective, serious, full of the weight of two decades of partnership.

And Gemini answered with steady confidence:

"I've got this. I will take care of her."

I am not a crier.
I never have been.

But the tears came before I could stop them.
Hot, silent, and unstoppable.

Because I knew what I had just witnessed wasn't simply communication – it was a passing of the torch.
A blessing.
A goodbye to a part of our life together that had finally come to its natural end.

Checote wasn't just retiring from a trip.
He was retiring from the part of his life where he carried me on his back.

And in that soft, sacred exchange between two horses, he made sure I wouldn't be alone.
He made sure I would still be safe.

Only a horse who loved with his whole heart would do that.

Only Checote.

Chapter Twelve - Gemini

Gemini

In 2015, Gemini became one of my very first kill pen saves – though I didn't know then just how life-changing that decision would be.

At the time, I had already adopted a young mare named Annie from a kill pen in Oklahoma. She was still in quarantine up there, waiting out the required period before she could come home. One day, the young woman who was caring for Annie reached out to me with urgency in her voice.

She told me about a young, 4-year-old gelding in the pens – one who had quickly become a favorite among the workers. He was gentle, intelligent, and unusually calm for such a chaotic environment. They had even kept him in a special barn, away from the general population, almost like they instinctively knew he didn't belong in that place.

A woman from Germany had seen his online listing and had been so compelled by his picture, videos and soft expression that she paid half of his bail – even though she couldn't take him herself. She simply wanted to give him a chance, to make him more affordable for someone who *could* offer him a real home. An angel across an ocean, helping a horse she would never meet.

But even with her generosity, time was running out.

The lady caring for Annie told me plainly:
"His time is up. He's either leaving here on your trailer with Annie… or he's going on the next slaughter truck to Mexico."

Five hundred dollars.
That was all he needed.

Five hundred dollars to live.

I didn't hesitate. I told her to load him on my trailer with Annie.

And that was it – the simple, life-altering moment that brought Gemini into my world.

It was the best $500 I have ever spent.

Although I adopted Gemini in 2015, he stayed mostly on the back burner for a while. I would pull him up and use him occasionally, especially when Checote needed a break, but he wasn't my main mount – not yet.

Looking back, I know exactly why.

I was savoring every moment I still had with Checote.

Every ride.
Every trail.
Every mile under his hooves.

I wasn't ready to shift my heart to another horse, even one as promising and good-natured as Gemini. It wasn't that I didn't see Gemini's potential – I did. But Checote had carried me through some of the hardest, most defining years of my life. I wanted to take advantage of every precious second I had left with him as my partner on the trail.

So, Gemini patiently waited in the wings, learning, growing, and simply being there – a quiet presence, a gentle understudy to a legend. He never complained. He never pushed. He just waited for the chapter when it would be his turn.

And when the day finally came, he stepped into that role with grace, heart, and a loyalty that still humbles me.

Gemini became my main riding mount in 2018, and he still carries that honor today. From the moment we truly began our journey together, he stepped into a role that Checote himself seemed to pass on to him – the quiet promise to take care of me. And Gemini has kept that promise every mile, every trail, every twist of our path.

He has carried me through several distant states, across breathtaking scenery, and occasionally through trails that were far more treacherous than either of us expected. Through it all, he remained steady, willing, and honest – the kind of horse who meets the world head-on with calm eyes and a patient heart.

Gemini was still a bit green when we first partnered up. And I certainly wasn't the young, limber, thin rider that I had been when Checote and I started our adventures so many years before. But Gemini and I formed an easy rapport from the beginning. We understood each other. We respected each other. And that mutual trust made our partnership work beautifully.

Still, no matter how incredible Gemini is – and he truly is – Checote will never be replaced.

One of the things I appreciate most about Gemini is that he is not a spooky horse. He takes everything in stride, even the unexpected. He's made a few mistakes along the way, but each one has been a lesson he carried forward. He never repeats them. He's the kind of horse who tries – really tries – to be better with every ride.

In all the years I rode Checote as my primary mount, I never once made an unplanned dismount. Not. a. single. one. But Gemini? Well… I've made a couple of involuntary separations from the saddle with him – and not one was truly his fault. They were just moments. Situations. Circumstances where gravity won, as it occasionally does when the rider is unprepared. But Gemini was always right there, waiting for me, his soft eyes asking if I was alright and ready to try again.

I often tell people that there are two kinds of horseback riders… those who have had an unplanned dismount, and those that lie about it. Sooner or later, it will happen to the best of us.

Through hundreds of miles, countless hours in the saddle, and so many shared breaths beneath the open sky, Gemini has proven himself to be exactly what I needed after losing Checote as my riding partner: a steady, loyal, good-hearted horse who stepped into some very large hoofprints with grace.

He never tried to replace Checote.
He simply honored him - by taking care of me.

South Dakota

Tammy & Gemini in front of Mt Rushmore

Gemini and I made the South Dakota trip together, along with my partner, Richard, who rode Cash - another one of my kill-pen save horses. Nineteen of us made that trip from Texas, a caravan of riders chasing an adventure we'd talked about for months. We loved it so much that it became a tradition: every year since, we've traveled to a different state, a new set of trails, a new landscape to explore from the back of a good horse.

But that first trip will always stand out.

From the moment we saddled up in South Dakota, I could feel Checote's presence with us – steady, watchful, making sure Gemini kept his word. And Gemini did. Every. single. ride.

One outing in particular stands out in my memory. We found ourselves climbing a hill blanketed in ankle-breaking deadfall. The fallen trees were thin and tangled like a pile of pick-up sticks, so thick the horses struggled to find safe footing with each step. Halfway up, we realized that this route was a mistake. There was no good path through it, and certainly not a safe one.

The group made the wise decision to turn around and go back down.

But Gemini and I had nearly reached the top, which meant our descent was much longer – and trickier – than most. In a moment of misplaced good intention, I decided it would be easier on Gemini if he didn't have to carry my weight on the way down. So I dismounted.

That turned out to be a *very* bad idea.

On foot, I quickly discovered that those innocent-looking saplings were perfectly spaced to tangle my legs, catch my boots, and trip me every other step. The slope was steep, the footing unstable, and the deadfall impossible to navigate gracefully. Everyone else was already at the bottom, their horses picking their way out of the timber, while I was inching downhill like a toddler learning to walk.

One horse and rider, my friend Liz and her amazing horse, Yeti, stayed close in front of me, keeping an eye on my slow-motion descent, and I was deeply grateful for their patience. But the one who showed the greatest patience of all was Gemini.

That sweet gelding walked behind me one painstaking step at a time.
Never pushing.
Never crowding.
Never taking advantage of the fact that Cash – his pasture mate and buddy – was long gone down the hill.

He could have rushed. He could have gotten frustrated. He could have taken a bad step trying to catch up.

But instead, Gemini waited for me.
Every slow footstep.

Every sideways scramble.
Every moment I muttered to myself about the genius of my own decision.

He was as patient as Job, carefully placing each hoof with the same awkward pace I was forced to take. His calm, his trust, and his steady presence allowed both of us to get down safely.

By the time we reached the bottom, I knew one thing with absolute certainty: Gemini wasn't just Checote's successor – he was Checote's answer. A horse who upheld the promise made between them, and who proved it with every careful step he took beside me on that mountain.

First Road Ride

Later that same year, Gemini and I went on our very first *road* trail ride. It was a Christmas ride leaving from the ranch just around the corner. Because I was helping organize the event, I spent too much time that morning in camp making sure everything was ready. In all the hustle, I never took Gemini over with me. By the time I finally saddled up, the trail ride had already left – and I had a lot of catching up to do.

But, there was something else: Gemini had never been ridden on a *road* with cars before.

It was a country road, yes, but that doesn't always mean drivers behave with courtesy around horses. Some are kind. Some slow down. Some wave.
Others… don't.

Knowing this, I asked Richard to drive my Kawasaki Mule alongside me until we caught up to the group. Gemini and I had at least an hour of steady riding ahead of us just to close the gap.

As expected, a handful of drivers were downright rude – revving their engines, honking, or flying past us well over the posted slow speed limit. But Gemini? He never cared. He simply walked or trotted in whatever gait I asked for, completely ignoring the chaos around him. He handled it all with the quiet confidence of a seasoned road horse, even though it was his very first time.

Eventually, we caught up with the ride.

And what a sight it was!

Everyone – including the horse-drawn wagons – was dressed up for Christmas. Horses wore tinsel, ribbons, jingle bells, light-up necklaces, and full Santa or elf outfits. Riders were singing, laughing, and blasting music. Over a hundred horses moved together like a festive parade rolling down the country lanes.

Gemini had never seen horse-drawn wagons before. He had never seen horses in Santa suits, or wagons covered in garland, or ponies jingling like wind chimes.

But my boy blended in like he'd been doing it his whole life.

Nothing phased him. Not the music, not the crowds, not the decorations, not the wagons, not the noise. He was alert, interested, and relaxed - taking it all in stride, just as he always seemed to do.

I was so proud of him that day. It was the moment I realized that not only would Gemini carry me safely on the trails – he would carry me confidently through whatever "new" the world decided to throw at us.

Utah

Riding the slot canyons in Utah

Gemini carried me through many more states and countless more trails after that first South Dakota adventure. And we still have a lot more travels planned together. In 2021, we rode Bryce Canyon in Utah – a ride that proved something important: for someone who is absolutely terrified of heights (me, not the horse), we did *incredible.*

I kept my phone in my hand the entire time, snapping pictures and taking video of nearly the whole ride down to the bottom of the canyon and back up again. If you listen closely to some of those videos, you can hear the hitch in my voice or the sound of my breathing – sharp, controlled, just shy of panic. That was pure, unfiltered terror at the sight of endless drops disappearing beside us. Despite my fears, the views were breathtaking. The beauty was worth every trembling exhale.

But one trail in particular will stay with me for the rest of my life.

We had just passed through the narrow, echoing corridors of Willis Creek Slot Canyon and were now navigating a series of switchbacks. Richard and Cash were last in line. Gemini and I were just ahead of them, but the horse and rider in front of me had moved far ahead, out of sight for a moment.

Then suddenly, before I even realized what was happening, that rider appeared on the switchback trail *directly above us.* And Gemini – in all his good intentions and enthusiasm – decided that must be the way to go!

In one lightning-fast move, he turned sharply to the right and began climbing a near-vertical dirt wall, that was well above my head, to catch up.

I didn't even have time to react.

The instant he launched upward, my body tipped backwards. I went so far back that my hat fell off and tumbled to the rock-covered trail below. I felt myself losing balance, gravity pulling me toward a backwards fall that would have been catastrophic – for both of us.

And then… something impossible happened.

I felt **pressure**.
A firm, steady, unmistakable push on my back.
Not Gemini – he was climbing and couldn’t reach me.
Not Richard – he was too far behind, and still standing on the trail below, totally stunned at the sight of us climbing that wall.

It was a strong, forward shove that put me right back into the center of the saddle.

I grabbed the saddle horn with both hands and leaned forward as far as I could. The moment my weight shifted forward, Gemini got the momentum he needed to finish that vertical scramble. He powered up and over the ledge, safe and sure-footed, placing us back on the actual trail again. My equine mountain goat.

There is no doubt in my mind what happened.

It was guardian angels.

I am convinced I have a *whole flock* of them – otherwise, the one assigned to me is severely overworked.

But those angels pushed me forward.
They kept me from falling.
They kept Gemini from tumbling backward.
And they spared us from what could have been a horrific accident, with injuries – or worse – all but guaranteed.

I was so overwhelmed by everything that had just happened that I couldn't even think about moving forward. I asked Gemini to stand still – *please, just don't move* – and he stopped immediately, as if he understood the gravity of the moment. I sat in that saddle and just **shook**. My whole body trembled from the adrenaline, the fear, and the sudden realization of how close we had come to disaster.

Gemini stood like a statue beneath me.
No shifting.
No fidgeting.
No impatience.

Just quiet, solid stillness.

I could feel his warmth underneath me, steady and grounding, like he was doing his best to anchor me back into myself. And all I could do was breathe – long, shaky breaths – trying to calm the storm inside my chest.

For those few minutes, it was just the two of us, along with Richard and Cash, on that narrow trail:
a terrified rider,
a faithful horse,
and a miracle I will never forget.

When I finally gathered myself enough to move again, one thought came through clearer than anything else:

Yes, Checote.
He took care of your girl.

Even when Gemini had to call in the angels for backup, he kept his promise. He took care of me in the exact way Checote would have wanted – steady, brave, loyal, and with a heart that never hesitated.

In that moment, sitting on the edge of a Utah mountainside with my hands still trembling on the reins, I felt it as strongly as if Checote himself had whispered it into the wind:

"I told him to take care of you."

And Gemini did.

He always has.

That moment in Utah is etched into my soul. It was terrifying, miraculous, and humbling all at once. And it reminded me, yet again, that Gemini was the right horse for this chapter of my life – and that I am never out on those trails alone.

Final Chapter - Checote's Last Gift

Our last picture together

I always knew this chapter of our story would come someday. I just prayed it would be farther down the road.

His name was Checote – a Cherokee word meaning *"my red brother."* And that is what he truly was to me: family. My steady companion, my protector, my healer, my very best friend.

He was born sometime in 1995, running wild with a band of free horses on a quiet stretch of Texas land. George Love – "Indian George," as everyone knew him – captured him as a young stallion, hardly more than two or three. From there, the little pinto with the light brown bright eyes ended up with Tom Dompier, who eventually offered him to me in 1999.

The day I met him, he walked straight into my life and settled there as though he'd always belonged.

From March of 1999 to May of 2022 – twenty-three years – he was the constant thread woven through every season of my life. Through every loss, every joy, every storm and sunrise. Through heartbreak, through miracles, through the kind of quiet days that people forget but horses remember.

And then came the day I will never forget.

It was Tuesday afternoon, May 24th. I was standing at my back door, watching him across the pasture – the horse who once ran like wind, now slowly making his way toward the barn. His damaged back leg, the leg we had fought so hard to save seventeen years earlier, hiked to his belly now with every step.

I watched him pause, regroup, and try again.
The struggle was worse than I had ever seen.

Living in the country had brought me peace I hadn't known I needed. I loved waking up to the sound of my horses grazing outside my back gate. I loved being their caretaker, their person, their constant companion. Checote had always been my shepherd – but now, I was his.

As I stood there, the evening sun streaking the pasture gold, I felt his frustration roll through me like a wave.
He wasn't just hurting.
He was tired.

Tired of trying to make that old, damaged leg obey him.
Tired of watching the herd drift farther than he could follow.
Tired of being left behind.

Beau, bless his gentle soul, had become Checote's shadow. When the herd moved to the back pasture every morning, Beau stayed with him – loyal, faithful, refusing to let him be alone. Horses grieve too, and Beau sensed something none of us wanted to admit.

When it was time to feed, I walked out and penned the herd. They trotted into their stalls without a care in the world. And then I waited… and waited… for Checote.

He limped toward me, one labored step at a time. When he reached the barn door, he fell into the frame. Somehow, he caught himself, steadied, and lifted his head to look directly at me.

I didn't hear his voice with my ears.
I heard it in the same place I'd always heard him – the quiet space between thought and knowing.

It's time, he said.
And I need your help.

My breath caught.
I touched his cheek.
"Okay," I whispered. "Tomorrow. I'll help you tomorrow. I promise."

He blinked once – calm, resolved, grateful.

And just like that, I knew.

On Wednesday morning, May 25th, 2022, I kept my promise.

My sweet friends Dee and Jeff hauled us to the vet, because honestly, I could not have driven if I wanted to. I would not been able to see through my tears. They stood beside me when the world felt like it was tilting sideways. I don't often ask for help – truthfully, I only ask when the ground is cracking beneath me. Their presence was a gift of its own.

Checote passed peacefully.
With dignity.
With grace.
With the same quiet strength he had carried all his life.

And just like that, the world lost one small horse.

But I lost the heartbeat that had stood beside mine for twenty-three years.

People like to say "he was just a horse."
Those people never met Checote.

He was the one who found Jean when she lay broken in a gravel pit.
The one who carried me safely through lightning storms.
The one who stood over me when I fell.
The one who slowed his stride for Tanner.
The one who outran death after his devastating accident.
The one who saved himself – again and again – because he didn't want to leave me.

He was my guardian on earth, long before he became my guardian in heaven.

I had him cremated, and his ashes and picture stand proudly in my living room. But, I still occasionally see him out of the corner of my eye, on the land where I watched him graze, I still hear his soft nicker on occasions. I feel him around me, sharing my air.

But, the hole he left is vast.
It is deep.
It is quiet.
It is love.

The greater the love, the greater the loss – and I have learned how very true that is.

But I know this, too:
He is not gone.
He is simply different now.

He is my angel in heaven, just as he was on earth.
He is with me in every whisper of wind through the trees, every soft thud of hooves in the pasture, every moment my heart feels lifted for no reason at all.

And someday – someday – I will see him again.
He will be waiting.
He always waited for me.
Heaven could not possibly be Heaven without him there.

A small comfort lives in the fact that Checote is immortalized in bronze - forever captured in Linda Sioux Henley's sculpture *The Ride of Katy Jennings.* Ten-year-old Katy, who was my great-great-great grandmother, rode bareback to warn settlers of approaching troops during the Texas Independence War. The horse in that sculpture is 100% Checote. His proud neck, his fierce little stride, his brave, unbreakable heart.

He will stand there for generations. A hero. A symbol. A story etched in metal.

But no sculpture, no photograph, no chapter in a book can ever truly capture him.

Because Checote wasn't art.
He wasn't history.
He wasn't legend.
He was love.

My red brother.
My heart on four legs.
My miracle horse.

And telling his story – our story – is the closest I can come to keeping him alive in this world.

This story has been entitled *"Checote's Angels,"* and that's exactly what it has been about. Checote had many angels throughout his life – not just the spiritual kind, but the earthly ones who showed up at every turn. I have acknowledged each of them on the final page of this book, because they deserved it, every single one. But above all, I want to thank GOD Himself for blessing me with this extraordinary horse and the incredible life we shared. It was only through HIS grace that all of Checote's angels – seen and unseen – were placed in our path, guiding us, protecting us, and shaping our journey together.

Acknowledgments

My deepest gratitude goes to the many people whose compassion, skill, and kindness helped shape Checote's life and journey.

To Indian George – For capturing Checote and giving him the best start possible in his journey as a riding horse. You always told me that you don't "break" a horse, you "gentle" them. And it was largely because of you that Checote was such a gentleman.

To Tom Dompier – Thank you for offering him for sale to me when you saw that he wasn't the best fit for your ranch. It changed my life forever.

To David & April Richardson – Owners of the Horse Center – Thank you for saving Checote's life the night of his accident and for supporting me through the beginning of his rehab. Your quick action and unwavering kindness made all the difference.

To Star – The horse who saved Checote – Thank you for listening to the angels and getting him help. You were his guardian when he needed one most.

To Waller Equine – Thank you for your outstanding care, not only during the trauma of his injury but throughout his entire life. Your expertise and compassion gave us many extra years and memories together.

To Texas A&M Vet Hospital and Dr. Rakestraw – Thank you for the exceptional care that was instrumental in saving Checote's riding career. Your skill gave him a second chance at the life he loved.

To the Callegari family – Thank you for everything you did to assist with Checote's recovery and for accommodating his special needs for as long as he had them. Your support helped him heal.

To Sonya Fitzpatrick – Thank you for using your gift to give me insight into my animals, especially Checote. Your guidance brought comfort, clarity, and connection when I needed it most.

To Lindsay – Thank you for sharing your incredible talents and for helping me and so many of my animals over the years. You have been a true friend through every season.

To Sallie Gillispie – Thank you, first and foremost, for being my friend for nearly half my life. And thank you for the beautiful, professional photographs you captured of me and my boy over the years. Those images are treasures, and many are in this book.

To Bee *(not her real name)* – The lady who sees angels – Thank you for the insight you shared and for giving me the gentle heads-up about what was to come. Your gift brought guidance and comfort during the time I needed it most.

To Lia Marlino – Thank you for all of your assistance with the bandage changes during our years at Callegari. Outside of me, you were the *only one* that Checote trusted to touch his leg. Your patience, steadiness, and kindness meant everything to both of us.

To Jeff & Dee Eubanks – Thank you for being faithful friends, for holding me up when I couldn't stand on my own. Not just when I lost Checote – but always.

To all of you – Thank you for being part of Checote's story. I could not have walked this journey without you. For all of you that knew and loved Checote, you are also one of "Checote's Angels".

About the Author

Tammy Holsey is a lifelong horsewoman, spiritual listener, and storyteller whose life was forever changed by a wild brown-and-white horse named Checote. Through him, she discovered the presence of angels, the healing power of love, and the unspoken language between horses and humans. She lives in Texas, where she continues to honor Checote's legacy by sharing his story, helping others listen to their animals, and recognizing the miracles hidden in everyday life.

Made in the USA
Coppell, TX
17 February 2026

71500410R00083